THE
ENCIRCLED
SEA

*A companion volume to the television
series produced
for Channel Four*

# THE
# ENCIRCLED
# SEA

## THE MEDITERRANEAN MARITIME

## CIVILIZATION

SARAH ARENSON

CONSTABLE · LONDON

First published in Great Britain 1990
by Constable and Company Limited
3 The Lanchesters 162 Fulham Palace Road
Hammersmith London W6 9ER
Copyright © 1990 Sarah Arenson
ISBN 0 09 469480 X
Set in Monophoto Apollo by
Servis Filmsetting Ltd, Manchester
Printed in Great Britain by
BAS Printers Ltd, Over Wallop, Hampshire

A CIP catalogue record for this book
is available from the British Library

*for Elisha,*
*who got me into the blue*

# CONTENTS

# ILLUSTRATIONS

## Colour

*ix*

*between pages 148 and 149*
A luxury cruise hotel (by permission of Epirotiki Lines, Piraeus)
The Greek archipelago seen from Delos (by permission of Mike Coles)
A Greek trireme (by permission of Mike Coles)
Raising a seventeenth-century naval gun in Israel (by permission of Kurt Raveh, CONRAD)
The Hellenistic ram of Athlit (by permission of Elisha Linder)
The Battle of Preveza, 1538 (by permission of Mike Coles)
Kotor in Yugoslavia (by permission of Yael Sneh)
A fresco on Thera (by permission of Mike Coles)
The temple of Apollo in Corinth, Greece (by permission of Mike Coles)
The Norman Capella Palatina in Palermo, Sicily (by permission of Mike Coles)
The Muslim fortress in Malaga, Spain (by permission of Mike Coles)
'The Sposalizio' by Canaletto (by permission of the Aldo Crespi Collection, Milan)
The fortress-church of Les Stes-Maries-de-la-Mer (by permission of Mike Coles)
'Portrait de Jeune Fille' by Picasso (by permission of the Musee Picasso, Paris)

## Black and White

# INTRODUCTION

Now, at the end of the twentieth century, the world resembles a small village in space, and the Mediterranean Sea seems to have shrunk to a lake, traversed from end to end by air in a few hours. Nevertheless, the civilizations which evolved on its shores shaped the history of mankind. Since prehistoric times, the relationship between man and the sea has been stronger around the Mediterranean than anywhere else. For this reason, the Mediterranean may serve as a living laboratory in which new ways of understanding and furthering that relationship can be developed.

In the past, man's impact on the sea and his deeds there were wiped out by the waves, leaving no more trace than the foam; but modern science and technology have given us the hope of finding the testimony to the past and the way to the future. A multidisciplinary approach is essential for this task, which may be achieved only by uniting the maritime aspect of many disciplines: geophysics and engineering, history and archaeology, anthropology and oceanography. Modern technology, such as sonar and underwater photography, diving and submarine equipment, is also indispensable. This 'humanistic oceanography' is the legacy of the pioneering Dr Elisha Linder of Israel, to whom this book is dedicated. He is the founder and moving spirit of the department for the history of maritime civilizations at Haifa University, which was the workshop for the formation of this project.

For many thousands of years this once 'great sea' has provided both a barrier and a bridge for the people who lived around it. New research is breaking down old barriers and building more bridges. While political, religious and racial developments still pose many obstacles, team-work and international collaboration are becoming an essential feature of marine studies, for no one country or body can deal on its own with the sea, common as it is to all.

For these reasons, a geographical, chronological or disciplinary division of the subject-matter of this book has been discarded as ineffective. The various

*1*

chapters deal with themes which cover the different facets of man's relationship with the sea, from fishing and other coastal industries to marine transportation, ships and harbours, naval warfare and piracy, navigation and migration, the myths and legends of the sea. Any real understanding of any one of them would be impossible without some knowledge of the others. Together they constitute a complete portrait of the unique contribution the Mediterranean has made to maritime civilization.

This comprehensive approach is balanced by the fact that in other ways the book is more limited in scope; it never wanders too far from the coast. It is not another treatment of the Mediterranean region in the wider sense, nor a treatise on the development of Mediterranean art and religion. Rome and Jerusalem, Athens and Cairo, Paris and Madrid will seldom be mentioned here. The decisions concerning the future of the Mediterranean may have always been taken in those cities, but the facts are being made elsewhere, in the fishing villages and commercial ports, in research institutions along the shores, in naval bases and tourist resorts.

The Mediterranean Sea, the focus of man's creativity for thousands of years, is being rediscovered. This book approaches a subject as old as civilization and as new as recreation. It is written for my fellow natives of the Mediterranean, who are privileged to live by this sea and share the responsibility for its future and ours, for the lovers and chance visitors to its shores, who come into contact with its rich and manifold life, and for those who may still be looking forward to an enchanted encounter with the Mediterranean.

The television series for which the research has been done captures the spirit of the material dealt with here. It is not an enlarged version of the commentary to the series, but a broader background for those viewers who would like a more comprehensive picture. Readers of the book will, in the series, enjoy a fuller personal and emotional experience.

I have tried to touch upon all aspects of the theme which seemed relevant to me, but there was no way in which any one of them could be presented in depth, and some omissions had to be made. This is a subjective treatment whose aim is to provoke further interest and study.

Details of the sources for quotations in the text which are not attributed there will be found in the Notes and Acknowledgements which begin on p. 193. The minimal reading list offered at the end of the book avoids all publications, however essential, which are written in languages other than English. It is only natural that in dealing with the Mediterranean most research and writing are done in the local languages: Spanish, French, Italian,

Introduction

Serbian, Greek, Turkish, Arabic and Hebrew. This self-imposed limitation made the lists somewhat arbitrary, but the bibliographies included in the works cited will lead one to further reading in other languages. In many cases, the works cited are quite old, but no recent English works have replaced them. Fortunately, the publications of the new international organizations, such as the United Nations and the EEC, are usually published in English.

In the use of place names, proper names and general terminology, the reader took precedence over scientific discipline. In most cases, the recognizable modern equivalent to an ancient name or term was used – Marseille rather than Massalia, Diocletian instead of Diocletianus and Calif, not Khalifah. In some cases, both forms are given.

Given the scope and nature of the subject-matter, this book relies heavily on the work of many people in various fields, and can in no way acknowledge this debt. However, special thanks are due to my husband Avie, whose common sense guided me throughout. The draft of this work was read by my friends Micha Livne, Assaf Oron and Dr Martin Levin, by Professors Trude and Moshe Dotan, and by Zvi Hermann and Paul Adam, both experts in Mediterranean maritime affairs. I am grateful to all these for their useful comments. The editor, Robin Baird-Smith of Constable, made my pidgin English readable and encouraged me through the exhausting last stages of the work. Thanks are due also to all the people and institutions who were involved in the project – any faults are entirely my own.

## CHAPTER 1

# AFTER TETHYS

T HE MEDITERRANEAN, the sea in the midst of Earth, is the heart of the Old World. The three continents of Asia, Africa and Europe converge upon its shores. This convergence is not merely a figure of speech; a line of volcanoes and incessant seismic activity, running from the Pyrenees to Anatolia, is its living expression. One may wonder why peoples dwell and prosper in areas where in living memory they have suffered catastrophic damage to life and property, as they also do in Japan and California. The answer is beyond the scope of this chapter, but some knowledge of the causes of this instability is one way of avoiding its consequences.

According to the theory of plate tectonics and continental drift, developed in the 1960s, the physical clash of land masses, the pull and push of ocean and continent, are literally the underlying causes of earthquakes and volcanic eruptions. Many millions of years ago, all present continents were one – the primordial Pangea – surrounded by the Panthalassa ocean. About two hundred million years ago, this super-continent split into two land masses – Laurasia in the north and Gondwana in the south – with the ocean Tethys separating them. About a hundred million years later, these two huge continents also broke up, slowly creating the present division of earth and water on our planet. This process was not ordered and simple; the plates broke up and collided again several times, but this was the general line of development.

During this long process, Tethys underwent many phases of expansion and contraction, differentiated by geologists by terms such as Palaeo-, Neo- and Para-Tethys. It finally disappeared, leaving the Mediterranean as a residue, a body of water trapped among great land masses. The continents continued to drift, with broken mini-plates revolving and regrouping to create the complicated shape of the Mediterranean coasts of today. They are still at work; Africa is plunging under Europe, Italy moves eastward, Turkey goes westward, and Arabia slides north along the Syrian–African rift, while a new ocean is being created in the Red Sea. The present Mediterranean is

3,800 km long, with an average width of about 1,000 km. Its eastern basin lies more to the south than its western part. However, this is just a temporary form, geologically speaking. It has been this shape for the short span of man's recorded history – the last five thousand years or so – and will probably remain so for the next few millennia.

Much of the evidence for these processes lies under water, even under the sea floor, which is being intensively studied by research vessels and submarines using sophisticated equipment and techniques; seismic reflection profiles, deep-sea drilling and conventional sampling are all cross-checked. Another part of the evidence is exposed, in the shape of high mountain ranges stretching along the coasts, active, dormant and dead volcanoes, earthquake zones and many islands. The young Alpine fold, formed only twenty-five million years ago, is famous for its marble, as found in Carrara and Marmaris. These are metamorphosed rocks, the result of heat and pressure transforming the buried strata. The rocks found in Cyprus, northern Syria and Turkey, ophiolites or coloured melange, are pieces of the deep sea bottom, and help to explain this complex geological process. Submarine mountains, the composition of the layers making up the shores, and the interface of land and sea are also clues to the geological past of the region.

In this general picture, many questions are still unanswered and several surprises await us. The Mediterranean is obviously divided into two main basins – east and west – with the Straits of Sicily between them. It is further divided into many inner seas, such as the Tyrrhenian, Adriactic and Aegean. When and why did these basins and inner seas take their shape? There is no generally accepted theory, but most scientists agree that the western basin is a much younger formation than the eastern. It is thought to have been formed as a by-product of the expansion of the Atlantic Ocean. Africa, which at the Gondwana stage was joined to South America far to the west of its present location, started to move eastward. As it approached the European continent, the mini-plates of Spain, Corsica–Sardinia and Italy rotated anticlockwise by some 20–40 degrees, forming the Balearic, Ligurian and Tyrrhenian Seas. Due to the intensive movements of the mini-plates in the west, there is nothing left of the old ocean floor.

In the east, the sloping edges of the continents are still piled up. The eastern basin has a floor of continental thicknesses, over 10 km in places, while the western one has the usual ocean floor, about 7 km thick. Some scholars believe the eastern Mediterranean is a residue of the ocean Tethys. Along the meeting-line of a continental mass and an oceanic plate, the latter, a

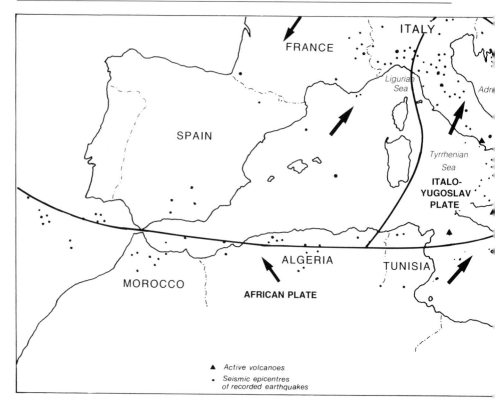

*Tectonic map of the Mediterranean showing plate thrust, earthquake zones and volcanoes*

heavier formation, thrusts under the former. At this point, a deep trench is usually formed, with an island arc framing it, and a closed sea in the centre. According to this theory, the eastern Mediterranean basin was formed on the western side of Tethys, behind the old island arcs of the present Greece and Turkey; the same process formed the Caribbean, South China and Tasman Seas. Consequently, both the eastern basin and the Alps may be seen as monuments to different stages of the dead Tethys.

The continental shelf around the Mediterranean varies greatly. Along most of the northern shores it hardly exists, while in the south-east it stretches for miles and carries wide sandy beaches and gradually declining soft bottoms. The gulfs or inner seas, like the Gulf of the Lion (south of France), the Gulf of Sirte (or Sydra, north of Libya), the Adriatic and the

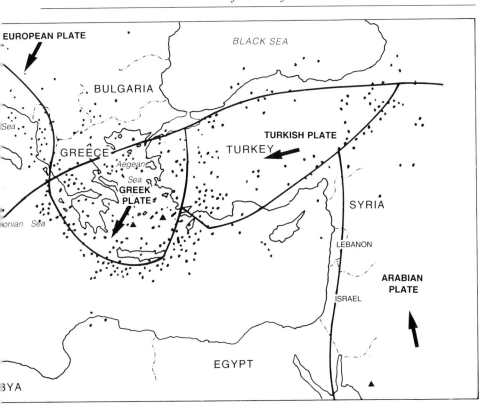

Aegean, are quite shallow and actually constitute wide continental shelves. The straits of Gibraltar, Bosporus and the Dardanelles, as well as the sills – raised ridges in the sea bed – which separate the various basins (as between Tunisia and Sicily), are only 100–400 m deep, while in places there are abysses reaching to 4,000–5,000 m (south of Crete, east of Rhodes, north of Sicily); these were created by the same process which formed the Alps. The continental shelf is essential for marine resources such as fish and oil, while sills and trenches are a critical consideration for the movement of submarines. Obviously, it is important for us to study all these phenomena; each is significant for some aspect of life in the Mediterranean.

One of the most surprising recent discoveries is that the Mediterranean must have dried out several times in its history. Geological understanding of the turning points in Mediterranean history reached its peak in the 1970s, the result of two drilling campaigns by the research vessel *Glomar Challenger*.

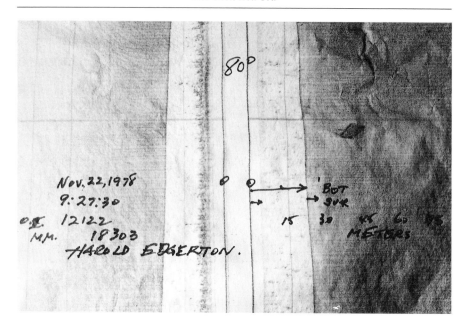

*A side-scanning sonar profile showing anomalies on the sea-bed*

The breakthrough was made with a reflection profile (a low frequency sound wave sent to the sea bottom to measure the depth and give a graphic profile), originally called Horizon M, which indicated huge salt heaps on the sea floor. Analysing the data, scientists concluded that the connection with the world's oceans at the Strait of Gibraltar had been blocked, evaporation had exceeded the inflow of water from the rivers running into the Mediterranean, and the sea had become a series of lakes, leaving a thick layer of salts which was more than 1.5 km deep in places and amounted to more than one million cubic kilometres. If the Strait of Gibraltar were closed today, the present Mediterranean would dry out in about a thousand years, and leave a salt deposit about 17 m thick. The sea was filled up again by a spectacular fall of Atlantic water over the Gibraltar sill.

This so-called Messinian Salinity Crisis happened within the last ten million years. It was probably triggered by an earlier event, the severance of the sea's eastern link with the world's oceans when a permanent connection between Africa and Europe was formed in the Middle East, around thirty million years ago. At this point flora and fauna started travelling along the land-bridge, while marine life began developing separately.

The salinity crisis may be traced in the special water system typical to the Mediterranean to this day. As it is a closed sea surrounded by land masses, and lies in the middle latitudes (39–46 degrees north of the equator), with the Sahara and the Saudi-Syrian deserts stretching almost to its coast, evaporation is very high (about 30,000 cubic kilometres a year). Furthermore, there is a dry season with hardly any rainfall for over half of each year, and droughts occur frequently. To this day, the rivers running into the Mediterranean do not compensate for the amount of water lost by the sea.

The water balance is maintained by a constant inflow from the Atlantic, in the form of a longshore current which goes east along the northern coast of Africa, north in the Levant and then westward along the northern shores; there are many subcurrents caused by obstructions in the form of islands and the contours of the coast. Another current, going westward at a depth of about 200 m, carries the heavy Mediterranean salt water into the Atlantic. These features all have a bearing on navigation, port building and other aspects of man's maritime activity.

Because of the negative water balance, the salinity of Mediterranean waters is higher than those of the Atlantic (38.5 parts per thousand on average compared to 36.5 parts per thousand), and the sea is significantly warmer (between 17 and 25 degrees on average, with local variations). In the winter, the heavy saline water sinks to the bottom, and the inflow from the Atlantic and the rivers flows on the surface. Sometimes these two currents clash, to form big swirls, 'gyres', noticeable in the Alboran Sea south of Spain. The mixing of the top and bottom waters is more complicated than in other oceans, and it takes about 80 years for the whole body of water to change completely. This unique water pattern of movement has great significance in relation to the use of the sea as a waste disposal tank; its study is essential if the international bodies concerned are to prevent pollution and keep the sea alive (see Chapter 3).

One branch of oceanography deals with sedimentology, studying especially the deep sea fans, a thick sedimentary wedge which often develops off areas of high sediment input at the foot of the continental slope, such as the major river outlets of the Ebro, Rhône, Po and Nile. A related field of study covers another aspect of these same river courses. The desiccation of the salinity crisis, as well as climatic oscillations such as the Ice Ages, caused major drops in sea level; the continental shelf was exposed and underwent deep erosion, proved by the gorges lying far up and down stream of those rivers, deep under the present surface of land and sea. Thus the

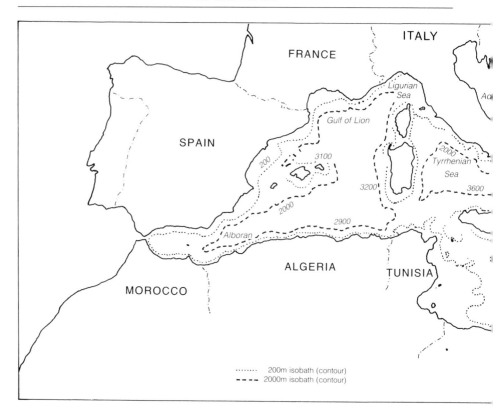

*Bathymetric map of the Mediterranean showing depths in metres and the principal Mediterranean basins*

Mediterranean, a multi-silled and almost enclosed system, serves as a natural sedimentation laboratory. The information gained from analysis there may be applicable to more open systems in the world's oceans, whose details are difficult to isolate and study.

Oceanography and the modern earth sciences have indeed contributed much to our understanding of the Mediterranean and the influences on its character. But these sciences have their limitations. Oceanography is based on present data, while most earth science research stops short at the holocene, the most recent geological era (around 10,000 years ago). This 'recent' past, of vital importance to our future, would have been a gap in our knowledge, if it were not for archaeology, which collates and clarifies our other information.

Vestiges of human occupation along the Mediterranean shores, especially

10

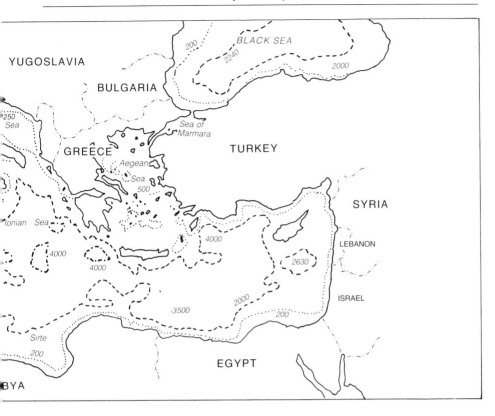

those which relate to the sea – ports and harbours, for example – are good indicators of the changes in sea level and the palaeotopography of the coastline. There are indications of sunken sites in some places, silted ones in others, with some exceptional examples of emergence or submergence; together these make a very complex picture. Sea-shells are one indicator, used by geologists to determine land–sea relationship: deposited by the waves, the shells usually lie with their convex side up, while shells discarded or dumped by man, usually from above, land on their backs, with their concave side up. Layers of shells at different levels can therefore mark either a previous coastline or a place occupied by humans. Another way of discovering sea-level variations is by the water marks in old wells, which are frequently found near the coast. Differences of sea-level affect the levels of ground water, which show on the walls of the wells.

A co-ordinated archaeo-geological survey of these coasts and continental shelves, pioneered by the Englishman Nicholas Flemming and now called MedSite, has helped to date and explain recent geological processes, and also to predict future developments to some extent. It is now estimated that, while the last Ice Age caused a difference of more than 100 m in the Mediterranean sea-level, during the last 3,000 years it has not changed by more than 0.5 m on average, although local tectonic differences made by the shifts of the plates could be as much as 5–15 m in places. In the south-west of Crete, for instance, the land has moved upward by around 10 m since Roman times, due to plate movements.

The most substantial evidence for the events of these remote periods of man's history comes from a recent excavation in Israel. At a distance of about 200 m from the shore, along the stretch of coast from Athlit to Haifa, a string of Neolithic villages has been discovered, complete with typical Stone Age houses built of wood and stone, including the remnants of foodstuffs such as kernels and bones, and the skeletons of some of the inhabitants. They date back to around 7000 BC, when, at the end of the last Ice Age, the melting of the glaciers must have caused a rapid rise in sea-level, and brought about the desertion of the villages, which became covered with sand. In this way they were preserved undisturbed, until the recent sand deficiency along this stretch of coast caused the exposure of these precious testimonies to the past of man and the sea.

This evidence adds to former discoveries of several submerged prehistoric finds around the Mediterranean. A collection of flint tools of the Palaeolithic Age (some 45,000 years old) was discovered on the continental shelf off the island of Corfu. The remains of what may be the earliest human structure yet known were discovered in Terra Amata, near Nice: an oval hut which had served as a temporary camp. Other settlements of the Neolithic period were identified in the Aegean islands of Melos and Aghios Petros. Against this background, man's first movements become clearer. Out of Africa, *Homo Erectus* spread around and across the Mediterranean in all directions. During the Palaeolithic Age he started to use fire and bury the dead. He was also fishing and visiting nearby islands in primitive craft, occasionally settling them. In the upper Palaeolithic era (35,000 to 10,000 years ago), progress was accelerated, with man's first attempts to art and agriculture. The Neolithic era has provided abundant evidence of the first permanent settlements, the use of pottery, the domestication of animals and of crude religious beliefs.

The cataclysmic events connected with the last Ice Age and the subsequent sea rise, accompanied by great changes in climate, flora and fauna, must have left their mark on man's collective memory. Indeed, in the creation myths of most Mediterranean people, the sea, or the great amorphous abyss, plays an important role. It is usually described as a negative, destructive power, a Goddess or God. It is known, for instance, in the Canaanite pantheon as Tihamat or Yamm, which is finally subdued by the good God, Creator of Earth and Man. The sea is chaos, associated with a series of terrible monsters – Tohu and Bohu, Leviathan and Tanin. In the Greek pantheon, the ancient sea-god Poseidon is a part of the new order of things, after he had deposed, together with Zeus and Hades, the old father-god Cronos.

The deluge, a universal myth found in very similar versions in Akkadian, Hebrew and Greek mythology, most probably describes an historical event. The terms go back to the creation myths:

> The same day were all the fountains of the great deep broken up, and the windows of heaven were opened. . . . And the waters prevailed exceedingly upon the earth; and all the high hills, that were under the whole heaven, were covered. . . . And all flesh died that moved upon the earth, both of fowl, and of cattle, and of beast, and of every creeping thing that creepeth upon the earth, and every man (Genesis.7:11 f).

After it had ended, the eternal hope had also to do with the water:

> And God spake unto Noah, and to his sons with him, saying, and I, behold, I establish my covenant with you, and with your seed after you; . . . neither shall all flesh be cut off any more by the waters of a flood; neither shall their any more be a flood to destroy the earth. . . . And God said, This is the token of the covenant which I make between me and you and every living creature that is with you, for perpetual generations: I do set my bow in the cloud, and it shall be for a token of the covenant between me and the earth. And it shall come to pass, when I bring a cloud over the earth, that the bow shall be seen in the cloud; And I will remember my covenant . . . and the waters shall no more become a flood to destroy all flesh (Genesis.9:8 f).

One of the main issues in prehistoric research is the explanation of the great uniformity in the development of life-styles and tools found in most Palaeolithic sites. Some scholars believe in common origins, which culture spread by contact and diffusion, while others hold that parallel evolution occurred independently, without the physical connections which are indeed hard to imagine at this period. But from the Neolithic Age there is definite proof of regular seafaring, so that similar phenomena may easily (although not necessarily) be interpreted by diffusion. In this respect, islands provide us with unique evidence. On the basis of the latest research, it seems now that all but the largest of Mediterranean islands (such as Cyprus, Crete, Sicily, Sardinia, Corsica and the Balearics) were not permanently occupied until the Bronze Age, or the third millennium BC. Settlement of the islands was not a matter of discovery (they had been visited and exploited formerly on a temporary basis), but a function of the survival rate of the population.

Only as a consequence of the agricultural revolution, the establishment of proper commercial networks and the development of adequate water craft, did the smaller islands become attractive for permanent settlement. Nevertheless, there were long periods of isolation, when indigenous culture went its own way. In the large islands of Malta and Sardinia, unique prehistoric temples, burials and towers (*nuraghe*) are found. These, and indeed a physical type which still exists may preserve what might be called the *ur* Mediterranean culture or aboriginal roots, as little untouched by outside influences as is possible in this melting pot of people and civilizations. Generally speaking, island civilizations are a microcosm where all the tides of Mediterranean culture leave their mark as they come and go; but it is also on the islands where one may find vestiges of the oldest Mediterranean traditions still in existence.

As we advance from prehistoric times, archaeology has more to tell us of the evolution of Mediterranean man and his involvement with the sea around him. Modern archaeology is only about 150 years old. With the discoveries in Troy, Mycenae and Crete at the end of the last century, Greek mythology was proved to have a historical basis. The Minoan scripts also discovered then have still not been fully deciphered, but another major discovery in the last generation throws new light on old legends. On the island of Thera (Santorini) in the southern Aegean, vestiges of a very rich centre of Minoan civilization have been unearthed: palaces and other dwellings full of frescoes, utensils and sculpture. These remnants cling to the mountainside, a part of a volcano which collapsed into the sea in what was probably the most dreadful eruption in human history.

The volcanic cavity of Thera was created by a gigantic burst around 1,450 BC, while the little island of Neo Kameni opposite is only about 200 years old, and still active. The effects of the terrible eruption may have included *tzunami* (huge waves), total darkness, death and pestilence, which were associated by scholars with the ancient stories of plagues and the migrations of the sea-people, which contributed to the fall of the great ancient

*The village of Su Nuraxi at Barumini, the most developed Nuraghe architecture in Sardinia*

civilizations of the Minoans, the Hittites and others.

Above all, Thera is associated with Atlantis, that legendary island described by Plato in his *Dialogues* (*Timaeus* and *Critias*). According to him, Atlantis was a very big island, consisting of a fertile plain growing all kinds of food in abundance, with a low mountain in its centre. Poseidon, who married the heiress of the island, embellished it by reshaping the ground into six concentric belts of land and sea alternately, and furnished it with fresh water and plentiful resources: metals and minerals, timber and wildlife, both plants and animals. There were bridges over the water stretches and channels through the strips of land, so that ships could move from the open sea into the acropolis on the central island. The whole complex was built up with walls, palaces and temples, coated with precious metals and decorated with statues.

It had a strong army and navy and an exemplary government. But with time, corruption set in: the people invaded Europe and attacked the Greeks, causing much suffering and bloodshed. Then, as Plato says, 'at a later time, there occurred portentous earthquakes and floods, and one grievous day and night befell them, when the whole body of the warriors was swallowed up by the sea and vanished. . . .'

Atlantis was sought in the Atlantic (the West Indies and Azores), in the North Sea, in the Tyrrhenian and elsewhere, but to no avail. In the last generation, several scientific missions have tried to prove, by underwater research, its relationship to Thera, but the mystery remains unsolved.

Vesuvius is perhaps the best known Mediterranean volcano. Its most famous eruption, in AD 79, wiped out the two Roman cities of Pompeii and Herculaneum, killing thousands of people but preserving under layers of hardened ash one of our richest sources of knowledge of Roman civilization.

Around the same Bay of Naples stretch the Campi Flegrei, the burning fields, in which Italians have enjoyed, from time immemorial, a natural 'sauna' made of jets of steam which they call *fumaroles*. Nearby, Stromboli is a perpetual torch lighting the sea lanes by night, while Mount Etna poses a constant threat to life and property in Sicily. Earthquakes continue to devastate Italy, Greece, Yugoslavia and Turkey, and to a lesser degree southern France and northern Morocco and Algiers. There is as yet no certain method of predicting their eruption although great advances are made yearly in this field.

Even today, then, dramatic natural phenomena have a profound influence on Mediterranean man's destiny. During the last century, after drastically changing the face of the earth, man has also started to interfere severely with the sea. But the sea is much more vulnerable, especially this enclosed sea. The construction of high dams along the main rivers has blocked the sediments that used to be carried into it, which causes severe coastal erosion. The Suez Canal brought new Indian Ocean species into Mediterranean waters, which disrupted the food-chain. The changes are most obvious around the deltas of the main Mediterranean rivers, but everywhere along the coast, deforestation, intensive cultivation, quarrying and reclamation are having a profound impact on the coastline and the water system.

When the first big dams and canals were constructed, the knowledge of the consequences was limited. Now it has become more evident. In Egypt, for instance, the Mediterranean is actually reclaiming the Nile delta at a rate of several metres every year. But new mega-projects are still being developed: the Moroccan–Spanish bridge or tunnel at Gibraltar, the Egyptian flooding of

*Skeletons preserved under hardened lava-ash in Pompeii*

the Qattara depression, the Israeli conduit to the Dead Sea.

When the effects of coastal changes are added to the alarmingly multiplying causes of water pollution, it is obvious that the time has come for a new reassertion of man's relationship with the sea. For the past 5,000 years, the Mediterranean has indeed been one sea, a well defined entity, with its parts interconnected and the whole under unique and intensive human pressure. During these millennia, the whole range of man's interaction with the sea has been created and developed; first the harvesting of its resources in fish, salt, and now oil; then the transportation upon it of essential raw materials, foodstuffs and luxuries; the development of the boats and the harbours needed for these activities; then the use of them as tools and bases for the domination of its expanses and shores, for migration to faraway lands. During all this time, man spread around the sea a basic stock of beliefs and ideas, a common way of coastal life.

The main challenge now is the preservation and rejuvenation of the Mediterranean and its common culture, through the awareness, ingenuity and co-operation of all Mediterranean people and the world at large. On all levels – national, regional and international – steps are being taken in several directions: science – the study of the problems and their possible solutions;

law – the creation of the legal framework for the prevention of destructive processes; policy – the establishment of long-range priorities and the solution of clashes between conflicting needs. The Mediterranean has become an international test-case, a model for problems that will soon arise in other areas of the globe which are less ancient and crowded. The Baltic and China Seas and the Atlantic Ocean watch the process and await the results. But first and foremost, the Mediterranean Sea is an integral part of the future of the people living around it.

CHAPTER 2

# THE FISH HUNT

FISHING IS ONE of the rare occupations in the modern world which is
still a primordial hunt. In Genesis, after the creation of the universe,
'God said: Let us make man in our image, after our likeness; and let them have
dominion over the fish of the sea, and over the fowl of the air, and over the
cattle, and over all the earth' (1:26). Having created man, 'God blessed them,
and God said unto them, Be fruitful, and multiply, and replenish the earth,
and subdue it; and have dominion over the fish of the sea, and over the fowl
of the air, and over every living thing that moveth upon the earth' (1:28).
Twice God orders man to rule over the fish of the sea; twice this heads the list
of all human occupations.

For thousands of years, intensive fishing has been practised along the
shores of the Mediterranean. Overfishing is only one of the reasons for the
fact that, although the marine fauna in the Mediterranean is incredibly
varied, this sea is relatively poorly stocked with commercial quantities of
edible fish. The variety of fish found there stems from the great antiquity of
the sea, from its range of depths and temperatures, and from its inner
divisions into ecological niches, while the limited quantities are caused
mainly by a scarcity of nutrients, due to the lack of a developed continental
shelf in some parts and to its special hydrology which causes an insufficient
mixing of its waters. Regrettably, the clear blue water of the Mediterranean
signifies not riches but a lack of nutrients.

From the fisherman's point of view, there are four main categories of
creatures in the Mediterranean Sea: the great mammals (dolphins and
whales), which are more the subject of myth than an object of food; the
demersal fish, the fish of the depths, such as the sea-bass, hake, and red
mullet; the pelagic (surface) fish, or *poisson bleu*, mackerels, sardines and
anchovies, as well as the tunny, which tend to live in shoals; crustaceans and
shellfish. As with all Mediterranean fauna and flora, each category includes
representative species from many regions, originating mostly in the eastern

*19*

Atlantic, but also in the Indo-Pacific, with many universal species as well.

The best way for the non-diver to meet them is to go to the fish-market, which displays daily, all year round, an amazing variety of fish and *frutti di mare*. Another good way to get acquainted with the fish is through aquariums and museums. The Monaco Institute of Oceanography has over a million visitors a year; this institution, with those of Naples and Barcelona, pioneered oceanographic studies in the Mediterranean and in the world at large.

But most people are happiest with fish on their plate – fried, grilled, baked, boiled, smoked or pickled, even raw. Though deep-freezing and the fast food industry have brought about a revolutionary change in prices and consumption habits, culinary history often repeats itself; this is true for Mediterranean fish, which are usually consumed fresh, as they have been since the time of the Caesars. The two Roman authors, Oppianus and Apicius, are practical guides to this day, if you like your recipes in Latin.

The number of professional fishermen in the whole Mediterranean at present is estimated at about 250,000, less than one in a thousand of the general population. In the past, fishermen certainly formed a much larger part of the population, even though some were on a part-time basis; most of the coastal inhabitants in prehistoric times lived off the sea. In the Neolithic submerged villages excavated near the Carmel range in Israel, along with many fish bones, the skeletons of humans were found which bore interesting evidence of having dived for fish; a distortion in the bones of the inner ear, a condition typical of professional divers. The ancient fishing methods – line, spear, trap and net – are still used.

Among these four major methods of fishing, the net was instrumental in making fishing a collective effort and opening the possibilities of a commercial, profitable enterprise. There are several main types of net; the drag (trawler) net, purse or seine nets and the entangling (trammel and gill) nets. Among these types, trawling is the most popular. In the Mediterranean, an otter trawl is usually used, with boards holding the mouth of the net open to the stream of water which flows through the net while the boat is sailing. It is dragged for a few hours at depths of 20–200 m, and catches the demersal fish and crustaceans. The net is lifted on board by cranes and emptied several times on each trip. The surface fish are caught in purse-seine nets, varying in size according to the intended catch, and operated from boats that are usually smaller than the trawlers. The expert fishermen identify the shoals and quietly cast the net, then close the upper part and lift it on board. Entangling nets are used in shallow water of 20–30 m. Commercial fishermen today also

*Coastal erosion east of El-Arish, a consequence of the Aswan High Dam*

*Fishing with a lamp in the eleventh century AD*

*Thera (Santorini): the inundated caldera formed by the biggest volcanic eruption*
*in human history*

*The tunny hunt in Favignana, Sicily*

*Spanish fishing boats at Tarifa*

*Aquaculture in Tunisia : raising mussels in a Tunis lagoon*

*The purple industry area at Dor, Israel*

*The Madonna with the Child and two Saints carved out of coral. It dates from around the end of the sixteenth century and is 10 cm high*

*Marine pollution in Caesarea, Israel*

*A reed raft on the lagoon of Cabras, western Sardinia*

*The reconstruction of a shipload of eleventh-century glass at Bodrum, Turkey*

*The Phoenician Tophet in Sulcis, Sardinia*

*Lifting part of the hull of the* Maagan Michael *wreck in Israel. The ship dates to the Persian period and may be Phoenician*

*Egyptian tomb reliefs c. 2500 BC showing ancient fishing methods:* (top) *encircling net;* (middle) *traps;* (bottom) *fish preservation*

use the long line, a system of hundreds of hooks, baited for different sizes and sorts of fish, even for large species such as the swordfish and the tunny.

Most of the equipment and methods have not altered much – boats, nets, hooks and ropes are still almost the same as those used in antiquity. The major change in modern fishing is the motor, used for moving the boats, for hauling the nets, for refrigeration and lighting. In order to attract the fish to the nets, fishermen often use lights at night. This practice was forbidden in ancient times, because of the danger to other vessels, which might be confused by the signals. In the past, fishermen believed that fish were attracted to music, but now they sing only to themselves. Baits and decoy fish, used by the ancients, are still in use today. Catching the fish by dynamiting the bottom, or using various toxins to paralyse them is unanimously prohibited but still practised.

Dating from as early as the third millennium BC, Egyptian wall-paintings exist which depict a lone man holding his fishing rod or casting his net in that beautifully harmonious gesture familiar to us today. Fishing was obviously a

*Dolphins on a mosaic from the island of Delos, Greece*

favourite aristocratic sport, and has continued to be so to the present day, although its appeal is now wider. In ancient Egypt, several sacred fish were never eaten, but buried and even mummified. Some of the ancient gods had fish as their symbols. According to Herodotus, Tyre was founded by the fisherman Ghuzos, and the meaning of 'Sidon' in Phoenician is 'the fishing place'. By salting and drying, fish could be preserved and marketed far and wide; in the Semitic world, a sailor (*nauta* in the Indo-European) is *mallach*, the man who engages in salting fish. Assyrian reliefs show the people of Ashdod and Ashkelon bringing tribute in the form of dried fish. The Jewish Talmud mentions more than 50 different kinds of fish, both kosher and non-kosher. Because fish spawn so many eggs, they became the symbol of fertility. Little fish are still thought to be aphrodisiacs. Pregnant women are supposed to eat fish, and women were advised to eat fish to increase their chances of pregnancy. Fishes' eyes, always open, are considered a good prophylactic against the evil eye. In the Magreb it is said to this day 'Fish on you' to ward off any trouble.

The New Testament abounds with realistic fishing scenes:

Again, the kingdom of heaven is like unto a net, that was cast into the sea, and gathered of every kind; Which, when it was full, they drew to the shore, and sat down, and gathered the good into vessels, but cast the bad away. . . . (Matthew 13:47–49).

This is probably a description of the purse net, while another passage refers to a standing net:

And he entered into one of the ships, which was Simon's, and prayed him that he would thrust out a little from the land. And he sat down, and taught the people out of the ship; Now when he had left speaking, he said unto Simon, Launch out into the deep, and let down your nets for a draught; And Simon answering said unto him, Master, we have toiled all the night, and have taken nothing; nevertheless at thy word I will let down the net; And when they had this done, they inclosed a great multitude of fishes, and their net brake; And they beckoned unto their partners, which were in the other ship, that they should come and help them. And they came, and filled both the ships, so that they began to sink. When Simon Peter saw it . . . he was astonished, and all that were with him, at the draught of the fishes which they had taken (Luke 5:1–9).

Although these scenes take place on the Sea of Galilee, a fresh water lake about 100 km east of the Mediterranean, they probably reflect fishing traditions which were common everywhere at the time. In 1986, the remains of what appears to be a fishing vessel were discovered on the shore of the lake, between Genossar and Migdal, dating from the time of Jesus Christ. It is no surprise that Christians readily adopted the fish as a sacred symbol; the letters making up the word fish in Greek – *ichthys* – were taken to represent the formula 'Jesus Christ Son of God the Saviour', which gave the symbol an added sanctity.

The classical world left us the first scientific works on fish and fishing, which begin with Aristotle. Although most of these sources tend to deal with the sensational and moralistic – the fishermen are always poor and miserable, the wealthy, cruel and corrupt – the information they contain is invaluable. Both Greeks and Romans preferred seafish to freshwater fish. In the edict of Diocletian (AD 301) seafish cost twice as much. The luxury fish were

*A fish mosaic from Pompeii (90 cm sq): the 22 species are all extant and identifiable, and most of them are still in demand today*

(1) *Electric ray;* (2) *Red mullet;* (3) *Grey mullet;* (4) *Wrasse;* (5) *Crawfish (in combat with no. 22);* (6) *Unidentified bird;* (7) *Rainbow wrasse;* (8) *Dogfish;* (9) *Sea bream;* (10) *Red gurnard;* (11) *Scorpion fish;* (12) *Sea bass;* (13) *Moray eel;* (14) *Murex brandaris (a whelk);* (15) *Blenney or goby;* (16) *Striped bream;* (17) *Smooth hound;* (18) *Scorpion fish (another species);* (19) *Shrimp;* (20) *Squid;* (21) *Two-handed bream;* (22) *Octopus*

24

sometimes brought to Rome by warships powered by oars. Authors like Cicero, Horace and Juvenal are full of rage and contempt for emperors and senators, who would pay more than 10,000 sesterces for a red mullet, and treat its cooking as a major state affair.

For the Roman aristocracy, fish and fishing became an obsession. Fish ponds were introduced from the East around the first century BC and were used both for growing fish and for recreational fishing. The remains of these *piscinae* are found everywhere, from Cyprus to Spain. They usually measure around 3 m by 4 m and are from 0.5 m to 2 m deep, with cells for breeding and hiding. The rich Romans used to boast of fishing from the rooms of their villas, even from their beds! They kept moray eels and lampreys as pets in their pools, decorated them with ribbons and jewellery and threw their renegade slaves to them.

These extravaganzas were the exception. The essential economic fact was the extent of the fishing industry, which must have constituted an important source of protein for the population at large. *Garum*, or fish sauce, was the equivalent of our cans of tuna, mackerel and sardine. There were many different kinds of this sauce, which was made with vinegar, oil, spices, and packed in elegant amphorae, smaller than those used for wine. There were fish-balls and fish eggs, a kind of caviar. Fish oil was used for lighting and as the basis for many medicines, while the skin served as writing material and was made into various vessels. Fish preserves were convenient provisions for the army and the navy.

The installations serving this vast industry are found from Crete to Portugal, but especially in southern Spain, where tunny and mackerel were used for the best fish sauce. Built of bricks and a special hydraulic cement (*opus signinum*), the installations were found full of fish remains. Fishing rights were a state monopoly under the Roman Empire, while the installations and the marketing were run by private enterprise. Stamps on the handles of the *garum* jars tell us the story of the great merchant class involved in the fish industry. The fishermen were free, but slaves worked in the industrial installations. The importance of the industry was such that the Spanish town of Abdera had its temple dedicated to the tunny fish, which also appears on its coins.

The Muslim presence in the Mediterranean left its mark on the terminology of the fishing tradition. In Spain, France and Italy, *almadraba*, *madrague* or *mattanza* are the terms used for the tuna catch, which involves a complex fishing process probably older than the conquests of Islam. The *rais*, or chief, is also the head of the fishing community. He used to spot the approaching shoals, organize the operation, announce the start of the festivities which celebrated a catch and preside over marketing and profit-sharing. Now sonar and aeroplanes are a substitute for the expertise of the *rais*, and the old tunneries are decaying, for Japanese factory boats receive the fish straight from the *camera morte*, the final part of the intricate net. The waning authority of the *rais* influences the whole structure of the fishing community.

To the occasional traveller, fishermen seem almost a nation apart. In Spain and Turkey, France and Morocco, Yugoslavia and Lebanon, fishermen have much the same faces, manners and superstitions. In their struggle with nature, in their mutual dependence, they share a common character and community life. Unlike the hero of the ubiquitous legend of the fisherman, his wife and the golden fish, today's fishermen are not necessarily poor; indeed, they are usually better off than the wage-earner on land. But they still face hardship, their families are under a heavy strain, and their community is not as closely-knit as in the past. While the individual fisherman would risk his life to save a fellow in danger, the newly organized fishing authorities cannot always find the right solutions for a bereaved family as did the earlier fisherfolk. Mercury, the guileful god and the fisherman's special guardian, is not as helpful as before, neither is St Nicholas as benevolent.

Although the Mediterranean catch is growing yearly, the individual fisherman and the fishing community are on the decline. Young people are leaving the profession – in France less than a third of the fishermen are below 35 years of age – and the old are not receptive to the necessary changes. In Tunisia, out of over 6,000 boats, only about half are motorized. Except for rare cases, Mediterranean fishing boats are small; usually they constitute a family enterprise, and the activity is carried on within the family framework. There is a constant tension between small-scale coastal fishing, which is the only source of livelihood for many families, and the larger co-operative trawler fishing ventures, which usually benefit far fewer people. Coastal fishing also comes into conflict with aquaculture and recreational fishing. Many fishermen have given up the struggle, and deserted villages are to be found all around the Mediterranean. In Portugal, the beautifully designed old fishing boats lie idle for modern economy and technical progress have introduced large ships in their stead. The old boats are sometimes converted to other uses, such as harvesting algae or seaweed from the lagoons. The seaweed is used for the fertilization of the adjacent sand-dunes, which are producing crops grown with the fruits of the sea. Another, more sinister,

*Roman fish sauce installations in Baelo Claudia, Spain*

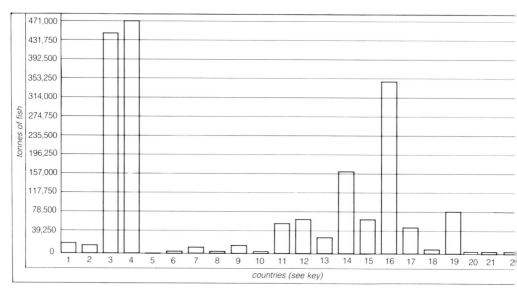

KEY

| Countries | Tonnes |   | Countries | Tonnes |
|---|---|---|---|---|
| 1 Bulgaria | 17298 | 11 Tunisia | 62853 |
| 2 Romania | 10374 | 12 Algeria | 64500 |
| 3 USSR | 450269 | 13 Morocco | 33208 |
| 4 Turkey | 469810 | 14 Spain | 160901 |
| 5 Syria | 923 | 15 France | 57690 |
| 6 Lebanon | 1400 | 16 Italy | 390414 |
| 7 Israel | 4072 | 17 Yugoslavia | 40489 |
| 8 Gaza | 1179 | 18 Albania | 4000 |
| 9 Egypt | 11208 | 19 Greece | 79062 |
| 10 Libya | 7425 | 20 Malta | 1197 |
|   |   | 21 Cyprus | 1556 |
|   |   | 22 Japan and others | 1011 |

*Mediterranean fishing catch by country*

adaptation is the use of fishing gear, from trawler nets to diving apparatus, to harvest a much more valuable treasure – marine archaeological finds. Fishermen, with their unequalled knowledge of the sea and its secrets, are leading this destructive occupation. Others, less adventurous perhaps, turn to fishing boat contests. The Cesenatico, in the northern Adriatic, boasts of the specially painted sails of its disused fishing vessels.

The rapid and intensive changes in land use and society have affected the fisherman's life in many ways. The Spanish Mediterranean coast, once famous for its quaint fishing villages and vast fishing activities, is becoming one continuous tourist domain, which attracts millions of northerners seeking its sun and golden beaches. When competing with tourism, fishing is the constant loser, for tourism-related enterprises are always more remunerative. It is usually the best workers who are lost first, so fishing communities have paid a high price for this boom in the national economy. In the wake of the developer's progress, centuries of skill and knowledge are wiped out, and ancient fishing communities become a source of servants.

But these are only some of the developments which have affected the Mediterranean. Factors such as overfishing, pollution and man's interference with natural phenomena have already had disastrous implications for the equilibrium of the food-chain in this sea, and have adversely affected the future of marine species: for example, sardines disappeared from the eastern Mediterranean after the completion of the Aswan high dam; oil streaks and other pollutants in the Gulf of the Lion directly affect the quality of fish in that region.

Another example of this disruption is the effect of the Suez Canal, which caused the introduction of alien species of fish from the Red Sea and Indian Ocean. This 'Lessepsian migration', now more than a hundred years old, adds new species to the Mediterranean every year and upsets the old ones. It does provide a unique opportunity to study problems connected with the survival of species, but on the practical level it creates problems. The Red Sea lizardfish, for instance, invaded the Levant Basin and established a population of considerable importance. Its expansion was at the expense of the other commercial fishes on which it preys and with which it competes, such as the hake; the dynamic coexistence between the lizardfish and the hake is affected by fluctuations in environmental conditions, to which the hake seems to be more sensitive. Some of these new species are toxic, and bring fresh dangers to a sea unaccustomed to this kind of peril. Recently it was discovered that poisonous sea bottom algae may have migrated from the Red Sea, causing tropical fish poisoning (*ciguatera*) to spread up the food chain. Deeply alarmed, there are those who would like to turn the Mediterranean Sea into a kind of nature reserve, where marine life will be protected from possible extinction.

The data needed for a complete evaluation of the potential fish resources of the Mediterranean are far from complete: it is difficult to collect and collate the information, for the places where fish are landed are widely scattered and often lack any statistical control. Evaluation is complicated further by the extreme diversity, in number and size, of the catch, and by the mobility of the fish. On the basis of this incomplete data, it is estimated that stocks cannot be developed much further. There is no point in attempting to increase productivity – maximum sustainable yield has been reached or surpassed in almost every sector of the Mediterranean. This problem is exacerbated by the nature of Mediterranean fishing, which is, on the whole, small-scale and diversified.

Scientific research into the fish resources of the Mediterranean was started by the Commission Internationale pour l'Exploitation Scientifique de la Méditerranée (CIESM), based in Monaco. The General Fisheries Council for the Mediterranean (GFCM) was established in 1949 by the United Nations Food and Agriculture Organization (FAO). Now we know that the eastern basin is the poorest, producing just half the fish caught in each of the western and central basins. Turkey is today the leading Mediterranean fish producing country, but only 20 per cent of its catch is from the Mediterranean; the Black Sea and Sea of Azov produce as much fish as the whole Mediterranean. Spain, France and Morocco carry on the major part of their fishing activity in the Atlantic. The Mediterranean annual fish catch is about two million tonnes, or just 1.5–2.5 per cent of the worldwide catch. Landings almost doubled in the twenty years 1960–1980, but this increase was mainly through fish caught in the Black Sea. Nevertheless, the population of the Mediterranean countries accounts for 10 per cent of the global consumption of fish, so most of these countries import a large amount of fish. Although the catch is limited, it is in high demand, and fresh fish fetches five times its average price in the rest of the world. The annual worth of the catch is about a billion dollars.

At present, the most effective way to organize fishing in the Mediterranean is by imposing various restrictive measures such as closed seasons and areas, a limit to the size and number of boats and nets, a system of quotas. One important restriction is a limit on the size of the mesh used in nets, to protect the juvenile fish until they spawn.

An important law fixes the three-mile zone as the limit for the trawlers, but this is often overlooked, and the shelters and spawning grounds of the fish are destroyed. In order to enforce the limit, submarine structures have been established, made up of old cars, tyres, wrecks and building debris. After a while, these became excellent spawning-grounds themselves. This gave rise to a new branch of fishing on these artificial reefs, which are becoming more and more sophisticated and specialized as their materials and shape are adapted to different fish and crustaceans, including the lucrative lobster.

Other restrictions suppress subsidies for boat building and establish catch licensing systems to prevent increased investments in fishing. Institutions like the FAO and the EEC are trying to build a working framework for these restrictions, which are very difficult to implement.

Enforcing restrictions on a fishing ground of close to three million square kilometres is an enormous task; fishing in the Mediterranean has turned into a hide-and-seek game between the fishermen, the police and the military. It is possible that satellites will soon be able to solve this situation by remote control, but in the meantime, only collaboration will help to increase stocks, and reduce costs by co-ordinating marketing, processing, etc. It is hoped that once collaboration is achieved in one sector, it will have a beneficial effect on other sectors as well.

While stocks of demersal fish can hardly be increased, this may be possible with the small surface fish, although unfortunately there is greater demand for the expensive demersal fish. Fish consumption around the Mediterranean is generally uneven. In most Muslim countries, basic cultural prejudices prevent the population from enjoying this local and cheap source of protein. Consumption is further hindered by the lack of a packaging and marketing infrastructure. In the Magreb, special efforts are being made to change these patterns.

Further projects concerning Mediterranean fishing are concerned with the development of the technology necessary for the design and construction of boats for industrial fisheries, including detection systems, the automatization of fishing manoeuvres, fish-processing on board, communications and navigational aids, ship and human safety, efficiency and comfort. Other projects deal with fishing ports and their amenities and with the marketing infrastructure, from refrigeration and processing to transportation and advertising.

It seems that the greatest hope for Mediterranean fishing is in mariculture. In a world endangered by population explosion, food from the oceans is becoming a source of hope. In the Mediterranean Sea, a relatively small body of water which can be more easily controlled, advanced and intensive scientific experiments in mariculture are being carried out. The time has come for the 'Blue Revolution', which will change fishing from a prehistoric hunt into a modern science, in which the breeding of fish and harvesting of the sea are planned and controlled.

There is no general agreement here either. Marine biologists and fishing experts would like to find simple solutions applicable to the fishing community at large. They claim that mariculture is the privilege of the rich communities, who can afford to invest in sophisticated equipment. They realize the difficulties of turning fishermen into hired labourers or laboratory farmers. But the general trend seems to be in that direction. One of the first successful collaborative efforts of Egypt and Israel after their peace treaty has been the cultivation in captivity of the gilthead sea bream (dorade), a little fish much in demand since antiquity. Egypt itself has greatly increased its fish production by developing aquaculture in its inner lakes.

While Spain is doing valuable work in, for instance, recording the fishing traditions of Catalonia, the real breakthrough lies in the aquaculture carried out in the lagoons of the Mar Menor and the Ebro Delta. France, Italy, Yugoslavia and Tunisia, as well as almost every other Mediterranean country, are investing considerable resources in developing this branch of their economy. The structures devised for growing mussels, breeding molluscs and raising oysters are a testimony to man's ingenuity and imagination. There are ladders and beds, leaf-like arrangements and tunnels, all made of durable and cheap materials like concrete and plastic. The possibilities of exploiting brackish water, lagoons and estuaries are just beginning to be explored, with very promising results.

The latest development in this field was the establishment of the Mediterranean Regional Aquaculture Project (MEDRAP) in 1980. Most developing Mediterranean countries are members, and there are three associated countries – France, Italy and Spain. This organization carries out pilot projects which have a major role in the development of aquaculture at the national level, and serve as training centres for experts and technicians from the Mediterranean as a whole. It has been recently calculated that, until the year 2000, world aquaculture production will increase at an annual rate of 5.5 per cent, to reach about 22 million tonnes, while conventional fishing will have an annual growth of only 0.3 per cent. The Mediterranean may contribute collectively towards this goal, especially through organs like MEDRAP.

The Mediterranean is one of the first areas of the world to have achieved some collaboration in the whole area of fishing, at the levels of research, administration, and actual production. But, as well as these achievements, the fishing tradition of the Mediterranean should be preserved, and the fishermen's intimate knowledge of the sea must be recorded, for the benefit of their own people and of all humanity.

CHAPTER 3

# THE WATER'S EDGE

L IVING AT THE WATER'S EDGE, man has learnt to exploit its resources beyond the basic quest for food. In fact, marine resources are just beginning to be tapped, and the sea is considered a major future asset. Almost every Mediterranean nation has its research institutions along the coast, collecting data from specially equipped boats or directly from the sea. Massive stone palaces in Monaco and Naples, functional glass and concrete boxes in Haifa and Athens, are connected to the sea by an umbilical cord which circulates salt water through the laboratories. Chemical, physical and biological studies of the water and its contents are carried out, and the sea bottom is surveyed extensively.

Naturally, the most intensive and immediate quest is for oil. Given the general wealth of the region in 'black gold', the potential for further discoveries of offshore 'ultimately recoverable' oil and natural gas is very high – particularly in Libya, where it is a hundred times greater than the general Mediterranean average. The recent discovery of offshore wells near Greece, Italy and Spain has sent other countries trying frantically to find their own sources of energy, especially those who are poor in any other natural resources, which includes many developing Mediterranean countries.

The production of oil and gas and their treatment constitute the heaviest industries around the Mediterranean at present. While future prospecting concentrates on offshore areas, the existing refineries cling to the coast for various reasons, such as proximity to the ports and the availability of cooling systems. These installations are the most prominent new additions to the Mediterranean coastal landscape. Most prospecting concentrates in areas with a wide continental shelf and has already initiated severe boundary disputes in this crowded sea.

The heavy industries around the coasts come into direct confrontation with another flourishing industry – recreation, which in its turn is

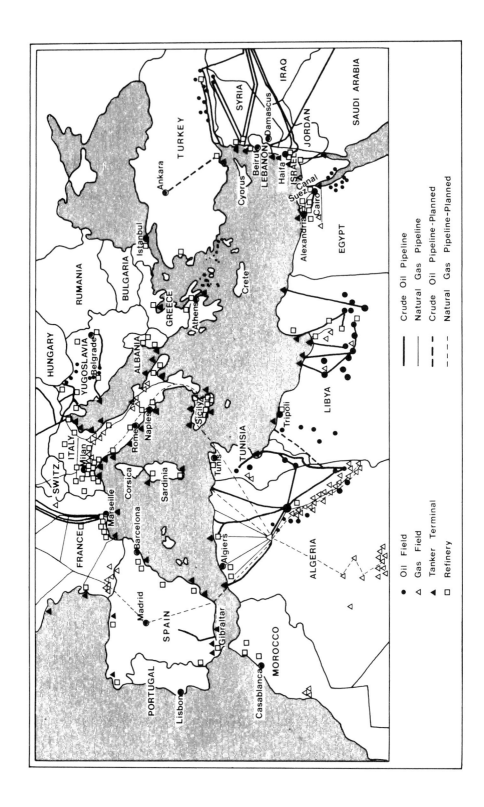

dependent on a good supply of energy. The energy-producing installations claim the same stretches of coast as the tourist resorts. Mediterranean countries have a population of about 300 million people, a third of whom live on the coast. These 100 million inhabitants carry the weight of their equal number in tourists, who flock to the Mediterranean shores each year from inland, from northern Europe and from other parts of the world. It is foreseen that in the 1990s, resort areas in the Mediterranean will have a density of three to fifteen people per metre of beach!

There are several variations on the theme of Mediterranean tourist resorts, from old towns turned wholly over to the tourists, like Sveti Stefan in Yugoslavia, to tourist colonies on reclaimed new land, as in Provence. Some old towns and fishing villages have been completely swallowed by time-share and high-rise hotels, while others have succeeded in concentrating development outside the historic settlements. Overdevelopment of recreational services, as in Spain's Costa del Sol, has harmed both tourism and the local population. In many other areas of the Mediterranean, the natives move inland during the summer months, driven out of their homes by what they consider to be modern waves of invading barbarians. While some places are forced to lay down a quota for tourists (no more than 200,000 a day in Venice), other areas with similar attractions are less visited. Thirty million tourists go to Spain each year, while only 300,000 reach Morocco, a few kilometres away. A positive by-product of tourism in many Mediterranean countries has been the redistribution of the population, by reinforcing the small littoral towns.

If large-scale tourism is considered by some parts of the population as a form of prostitution, traditional small-scale prostitution is still an inseparable part of life by the sea. The oldest profession thrives in the ports, where mariners still go ashore looking for their faraway home. The Red Street of Ephesos, over 2,000 years old, with its notorious Aphrodite temples, has its equivalents wherever sailors land for refreshment.

Side by side with the oil wells and the refineries, with tourist resorts and their amenities, ancient industries thousands of years old are still being pursued. The sea has always been the largest source of salt production for human consumption. Although usually inexpensive, salt is a prime necessity and thus, when scarce, could in the past reach very high prices and even turn into an accepted currency. It has always been a good source of revenue for the

*Oil and gas installations around the Mediterranean*

*The three dominant muricid species used for the ancient Mediterranean dyeing industry.*

authorities who levied taxes on it. Apart from routine consumption, salt was, in pre-refrigeration days, essential for the preservation of food, especially of high protein nutrients like fish and meat. Today, salt is used with its derivatives for a multitude of purposes, from fertilizers and insecticides to preservatives and cosmetics.

In times past, this vital commodity was the source of affluence for some great sea powers such as Phoenicia and Venice. An interesting theory considers the production of salt as an indicator for the rise and fall of ancient civilizations. When sea-level changes affected the salt pans, the industry collapsed and alternative sources had to be found. One explanation of the political and economic pact between Hiram, King of Tyre, and Solomon, King of Israel, cites the deterioration of Phoenician salt-production and the need to develop the Dead Sea works. Similarly, the ups and downs of early Venetian history were probably conditioned by the salt production of its own lagoons, as well as that of its possessions overseas.

Until recently salt pans in Cyprus, Sicily and the Camargue were harvested by women, and donkeys carried the produce. Windmills were sometimes used to pump the water, and they still make a pretty sight amidst the sun-scorched pans. The salt is arranged in shining white cones, which may be covered by tiles to help it last until it is marketed. Salt extraction demands not only expertise in deciding the exact level of the pans and the slope of the channels for the brine and in regulating the works according to the evaporation rates, but also hard labour in the hottest summer months. However, in most cases, salt production around the Mediterranean is now thoroughly industrialized.

The production of purple dye may have been the second oldest coastal industry. Like salt production, it was at the basis of the Phoenician maritime economy. 'Born to purple' (*porphyrogenitos* in Greek) means royal. But how was purple born? The ancients had to use natural dyes to colour their materials, which were also made from natural fibres – wool, linen, cotton and silk. Most natural dyes, such as indigo and ochre, lose their original gloss with continuous exposure to the sun and water. There was only one dye that was bright and stayed that way, especially on silk and wool; it was all the shades from violet to light blue. This was *purpura* or purple, considered the utmost luxury. In the Song of Solomon (3:9–10):

> King Solomon made himself a chariot of the wood of Lebanon. He made the pillars thereof of silver, the bottom thereof of gold, the covering of it of purple, the midst thereof being paved with love, for the daughters of Jerusalem.

Purple dye was probably discovered and perfected by fishermen, whose boats and clothing became terribly stained by the murex shells crushed by chance. Natural purple is a minute secretion of a small gland of the mollusc inside its shell. It is probably produced by the snail for defensive reasons, but may be extracted and collected, though not more than once, from the live snail. One gram of pure purple was made from about 8,000 snails, and today would cost about £4. In order to dye one kilogram of wool or silk, about 30 grams of pure purple would be needed. It was therefore worn only by the aristocracy and the priesthood, then by royalty and members of the Church. Jewish *taliths* (prayer shawls), Roman *togas* and Church *pallia* (ceremonial robes) were decorated with purple stripes, or dyed purple.

The dyeing process involved great quantities of water, both saline and sweet, the flow of which had to be controlled in a well-organized system of pools. The best location for these would be a flat, rocky beach, preferably of soft beach-rock, with a good supply of fresh water not far inland. Some of these sites grew into sizeable towns, providing the necessary labour as well as the port facilities for the export (and import) trade. However, traces of the industry are found also in small, isolated settlements. In many Minoan, Phoenician and Punic sites around the Mediterranean, vestiges of the purple dye industry have been found in the form of discarded shell-heaps, dyeing pools and traces of the dye in clay jars.

It is now proven that the Minoans knew the secret of purple dye, but the Phoenicians were the first to turn this industry into a prosperous international business. This was the root of their name in Greek: in the East they were known as Canaanites. In the Roman Empire, the purple dye industry was highly controlled, and later became a state monopoly in the Byzantine and Muslim Empires. It is curious to learn of Christian ecclesiastical purple robes lined with verses from the Koran, simply because the Muslim Tiraz workmanship was irresistible. In the later Middle Ages, purple was displaced by *kermes*, the crimson dye produced from an insect that thrives on the Mediterranean oak tree. Later on, with the introduction of chemical dyes, the secret of its production was lost.

Both the archaeological remains and the literary sources tell us of the importance of this industry, but the exact process is still a mystery. How did they catch all those snails? Where did they store them? How did they keep them alive? What exactly were the different stages of production? The Centre for Maritime Studies at Haifa University is conducting research into this.

Today's sponge divers are the last exponents of yet another ancient Mediterranean tradition. Their intimate knowledge of the sea, and especially of the sea bottom, is unsurpassed, but cheaper synthetic products are cutting off their livelihood, and the prospects for the future of their profession are dim. For centuries, they have been free-divers, performing amazing feats underwater. However, few men reached old age and, among those, few were not crippled by divers' diseases. Today only a few youngsters are trained as sponge divers, mainly in Turkey and Tunisia. It seems they are attracted less to the sponges than to the illegal trade in underwater antiquities, a much more profitable commodity.

The sponges are now sought for their scientific value, since the rate of their growth and their distribution are good indicators of the oxygen level and other qualities of the seawater. There are new methods of measuring and photographing them *in situ*, by remote control. These studies have already demonstrated critical shortages of oxygen; similar critical shortages were previously known in the northern Adriatic several times between 1977 and 1989. They have also shown that the revival rate of the sponges is much faster than previously thought – within a few years the sponge population recovers quite well.

Coral is much more valuable but, as in the case of pearls (which are not to be found in Mediterranean waters), the synthetic industry has almost done away with the ancient craft. In addition, coral is now protected by law all over the Mediterranean, because of its scarcity, due to hitherto uncontrolled exploitation. Coral today is collected in a much more rational way, without undue damage and with an eye to future growth. In this case also it was found that coral grows much faster than previously thought. The traditional centres of coral production, especially in the southern Tyrrhenian Sea, with the 'capital' in Torre del Greco, are still quite active. Side by side with the old-style necklaces and rosaries, crosses and Madonnas, new artistic creations in coral enliven both this cottage industry and the sculptors' work.

The high price of coral allows the divers to use modern equipment, but they use it according to their own adventurous code, often disregarding both instructions and safety rules. Jacques Mayol has demonstrated the unbeliev-able possibility of free diving (on one inhalation of air) to depths of around 100 m, for three to four minutes at a time. In the same spirit, the new generation of coral divers are using their own mixture of compressed air and helium, which enables them to stay longer at greater depths, with a big saving in expense. Their methods are closely monitored by physicians who specialize in hyperbaric medicine which studies the effects of submersion on humans; there are new possibilities in this field. (See Appendix D.)

Another coastal resource which has been tapped on a large scale since antiquity is building materials. On coasts and beaches these are plentiful, and have the added attraction that they are easy to transport. The principal building material (besides bricks) around the Mediterranean has always been stone, often quarried along the coast out of various types of beach-rock and sand-stone, but also of limestone and marble. This was easily transported by means of rafts to serve in the construction of nearby towns and harbour sites. The sites of the quarries were later used for other purposes, such as docks, fish ponds, industrial tanks (as for dyeing) and warehouses. These quarries are an important indicator of changes in sea-level through the ages, although research into their typology and chronology is just at its start. A French team associated with the Centre National de la Recherche Scientifique (CNRS) and headed by Paolo Pirazzoli has conducted pioneering investigations of this sort around Marseille and the nearby quarries of La Couronne and at other sites in the north-west Mediterranean, while parallel research is being carried out in the eastern Mediterranean, on the coasts of Israel and Turkey. Later in history, the old towns themselves became stone quarries – Acre was rebuilt in the Ottoman period with ashlar blocks transported on rafts from Roman

Caesarea and Crusader Athlit. The monumental Roman buildings in Provence have supplied building material for centuries, wherever there was a convenient waterway to carry them away.

The coasts are also the largest source of sand and gravel for the building industry, now based mostly on concrete in its different forms. As an essential component of concrete, huge quantities of sand and gravel are carried away from the beaches, transforming their shape. Since most of the bigger rivers that flow into the Mediterranean are now dammed, only a minimal amount of silt is carried down to the sea. Coastal erosion, aggravated by quarrying operations, is becoming a major problem, especially along the south and eastern coasts. These are the coasts of the developing countries of the Mediterranean, whose governments are faced with difficulties in deciding their order of priorities; laws forbidding unauthorized quarrying along the coasts are often hard to pass and to enforce, because of the pressure for housing and development.

Concrete was known to the Romans, who used a special hydraulic type for marine construction and for installations connected with water, such as water tanks and aqueducts. In its preparation, they used cement made of pumice or volcanic ash, which they mixed with lime and pebbles or potsherds, creating a most durable building material. This special cement is still known by the trade name Pozzolana, after Pozzuoli (Roman Puteoli), a port town in the Bay of Naples, at the foot of Mount Vesuvius, but now it is usually made synthetically. On volcanic islands scattered by the dozen around the Mediterranean, quarries of pumice and volcanic ash several metres thick are still the main source of revenue for the inhabitants. Material from the island of Thera was used in the last century for the construction of the Suez Canal.

The very fine sand found in several places around the Mediterranean was essential in the manufacture of glass, the invention of which was previously attributed to the Phoenicians. In fact, they learnt it from Egypt and Mesopotamia, but perfected its manufacture and made it famous all over the Mediterranean. They used the cold-cut and sand-and-clay-core techniques while their speciality was small faience objects, with vivid colours and fanciful designs. Only from the first century BC was blown glass commercially made; glass mirrors became common, and glass became generally clearer and crystal-like; most pre-Roman glass objects imitated precious and semi-precious stones and were colourful rather than clear and transparent. Glass artists from the Phoenician period onward used to sign their work, and some of these names have reached us. Ariston, for example, who specialized in blue glass, and Ennion, who inscribed his vessels with the words 'Ennion made this, the buyer should know!'.

Because of its fragility, ancient glass is found on land mostly in funerary contexts. At sea, it is found best preserved in shipwrecks. Recent underwater discoveries of glass throw new light on obscure periods in Mediterranean history; in Kaş, southern Turkey, for instance, a fourteenth-century BC wreck contained glass ingots as part of the cargo. Not far from Kaş, in Serçe Liman, scientists are reconstructing the hull of a ship dating from the eleventh century AD, probably of Byzantine origin, which carried an unusual cargo – mainly glass vessels of the highest quality and workmanship, made in the Shi'ite Califate of the Fatimids, which was centred in Cairo. There were cups and tumblers, bottles and beakers, and beside the whole objects, there was about half a tonne of cullet (waste glass) in heavy chunks, ranging in colour from blue and green to amber and crimson, and over two tonnes of broken glass, which practically filled the hull of the ship. There were also glass balance-weights and glass jettons, as well as ceramic vessels (some of them glazed), metal objects such as anchors, buckets, weapons and coins. A good part of the hull of the ship was preserved. While some of the finds bear Greek graffiti, others are inscribed in Arabic, deepening the mystery of the boat's origin, the crew's composition and the destination of the voyage.

The tradition of glass-making remained strong in the eastern Mediterranean when the Crusaders came to control parts of the Levant in the twelfth and thirteenth centuries; these skills were carried by the Europeans to their places of origin. This is perhaps how Tyrian glass reached Venice, and then Murano. The secret of Venetian 'maritime glass' lay in the use of fine coastal silica combined with soda ash made of burnt seaweed, both from locations in its eastern Mediterranean maritime empire. The products of the Murano factory, in the form of glass beads and imitation jewellery, became the favourite treasure carried by travellers to the Far East (including Marco Polo on his way to China). Artisans trained in Venice laid the foundations of northern European production, which attained an artistic peak in the stained glass church windows of the Gothic period.

Soap was another Mediterranean product which depended on seaweed soda ash as an essential ingredient. Made with olive oil, the soap produced around the Mediterranean was light in colour, hard in texture, and had a fine smell, while European continental soaps were soft, dark and foul-smelling because of their ingredients – tallow and animal fats. Until the fourteenth century, Spain was the leading exporter, then Venice joined the race by importing the soda ash from its eastern Mediterranean empire. This relatively

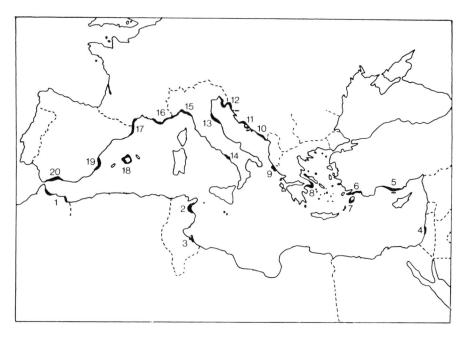

*The main recreation areas around the Mediterranean*

(1) *Morocco – Al Huceima;* (2) *Tunis – Gulf of Hammamet;* (3) *Djerba;* (4) *Israel;* (5) *Gulf of Antalia;* (6) *Marmaris;* (7) *Rhodes;* (8) *'Apollo coast' and the Saronic Gulf islands;* (9) *Corfu (Kerkyra);* (10) *Montenegro;* (11) *Dalmatian Riviera;* (12) *Istria;* (13) *Emilia-Romagna;* (14) *Costa Amalfitana;* (15) *Italian Riviera;* (16) *French Riviera;* (17) *Cote Vermeille and Costa Brava;* (18) *The Barearic islands;* (19) *Costa Blanca;* (20) *Costa del Sol*

heavy cargo provided useful ballast for ships carrying light and bulky cotton and the luxury spices. By the fifteenth century, western soap was sold to the East, where it was first developed.

The twelfth and thirteenth centuries were a watershed in the history of Mediterranean technology. For two to three thousand years, since the first contacts were established, the eastern Mediterranean had exported to the western basin all manner of sophisticated finished products in return for raw materials like metal and timber, and slaves. From the Renaissance on, the East deteriorated under Turkish rule, while the West developed its technological superiority. The shift of Mediterranean industrial activity from the south-east to the north-west, a movement which started at the end of the Middle

Ages, is the single most crucial factor in the region's economic situation today.

The remedies to the problems of the Mediterranean lie beyond the scope of this chapter. As to the future of the coastal industries, research has just begun into the further use of marine resources. One of the most promising fields of marine industry is pharmacology. Medicines and diets based on marine products may constitute an answer to the ailments of modern man and form a substitute for conventional pharmacology. The once ubiquitous cod liver oil is now supplemented by an assortment of preparations made from fish and seaweed, some of which could change our whole approach to medical treatment in the future. Genetic and other medical research is turning more and more to experiments on sea creatures and plants. Unusual sugars, polysaccharides, chitin, a waste product of aquaculture, and new toxic substances are all being tested for commercial production.

The Mediterranean is the first place in which submarine freshwater springs are being commercially exploited. These springs are generally located off arid lands. They discharge large quantities of valuable water into the sea, and may turn out to be of great help to drought-stricken Mediterranean regions. Desalination projects, the more conventional approach to the same problem, have proved to be an economic disappointment because of the cost of the energy involved, but new methods are being constantly tested.

The Mediterranean can also be treated as a potential energy producer, both from wave energy and as a huge reservoir of solar-heat. The chemical and mineral qualities of the water are just beginning to be evaluated. As part of an international venture, polymetallic sulphides, cobalt and manganese crusts and nodules are being explored on the sea-bottom.

Meanwhile, the Mediterranean has a passive role as the waste dump for all the activities around its shores. Because of the special water system of the Mediterranean, it is highly vulnerable to pollution. The geophysical facts, combined with intensive human activity, caused its ecological problems to become apparent earlier than elsewhere. Since the beginning of the 1970s, when the United Nations Environment Programme (UNEP) turned its attention to these problems and institutionalized its intentions in the Barcelona Convention of 1975, great advances have been made. 17 Mediterranean countries and the EEC have signed the convention, and Albania is now also showing interest. The Mediterranean Action Plan (MAP), approved at the Barcelona convention, aims at combating pollution by monitoring, research and by co-operative action, and at planning the development and management of the resources of the Mediterranean region by integrated collaborative measures (see Appendix A).

One of the major problems facing the implementation of MAP is the gap which exists between the northern and southern Mediterranean countries, especially in matters of research and development. A new Mediterranean Centre for Research and Development in Marine Industrial Technology was pioneered by Elizabeth Mann-Borgese and established in 1988 in Malta, to bridge this gap, and to promote the transfer of marine technology and its promulgation among all interested countries through educational and training programmes. The developed countries of the north-western Mediterranean, which create most of the pollution problems, are trying by this means to contribute to the interests common to all the Mediterranean, as well as making an effort to control their own economies.

The first stage – collecting the data and searching for the best solutions – is over. The time has come to decide the order of priorities and to act accordingly. As a senior official of UNEP has stated: 'We should not seek to co-operate on mere marginal issues. Some may think that it is easier to agree on such issues . . . but this is a short-sighted attitude. The fact that the issue is marginal . . . will weaken the chances of co-operation. . . . We should take the bull by the horns. . . .' The Mediterranean countries have to plunge into the deep, instead of treading water.

One direct and constructive outcome of these efforts has been the measure of collaboration achieved among nations which otherwise have little in common. Dealing with the problems of the Mediterranean has been the first large-scale project to demonstrate that hopeful international decisions could be transformed into meaningful action. The experience gained in the Mediterranean has served as a model for the foundation of the worldwide Regional Seas Programme, which co-ordinates similar activity in ten other regions and involves about 130 coastal states around the world. Several sub-regional activities have sprouted out of the overall plans, and are carried out by countries which otherwise do not fully co-operate with each other; RAMOG, for instance, a joint project of France, Italy and Monaco, studies the Ligurian Sea; there is an Adriatic project involving Italy and Yugoslavia, and an Ionian project shared by Italy and Greece. Further areas are being considered for regional co-operation, such as the Sicilian straits between Tunis, Sicily and Malta. It is to be hoped that other Mediterranean countries will also rise above their feuds and traditional hostilities to deal with mutual problems which cannot be solved without the co-operation of all who live around the oldest industrial sea in the world.

CHAPTER 4

# THE WAY OF A SHIP

There be three things which are too wonderful for me, yea, four which I
know not: The way of an eagle in the air; the way of a serpent upon a
rock; the way of a ship in the midst of the sea; and the way of a man with a
maid                                                                (Proverbs 30, 18–19).

N AVAL ARCHITECTURE is one expression of man's reaction to a
complex challenge which combines natural forces, raw materials,
economic interests, social and political pressures. It is a cultural indicator
and, as such, is a subject central to the search into the past and a reflection of
present conditions.

Sea-going vessels developed around the world on similar lines, but it was
the Mediterranean tradition that served as the basis for modern developments. Our generation may be the last witness to this tradition, which goes
back thousands of years and still lingers on precariously in the small
shipyards of the Aegean islands, in the *squeri* of Venice, in Malta and in Syria.
Since the materials and tools, the techniques and methods of construction
used are very old, one may still find the answers to questions which concern
the distant past. What goes into the building of a ship? Are plans and
calculations a part of it? How long does it take? What is the cost?

Although the basic challenge is always the same – volume, durability,
security and speed, balanced by low costs of materials and labour – it is
obvious that a modern shipyard cannot serve us as a reference. Here,
everything is different – the careful design and engineering; the scientific
calculations and drawings; the mass production of components, mainly made
of steel; the motorized power, which influences the whole structure. This
new kind of ship is the product of the industrial revolution, rather than a
descendant of the past; there is no comparison in tonnage, design,

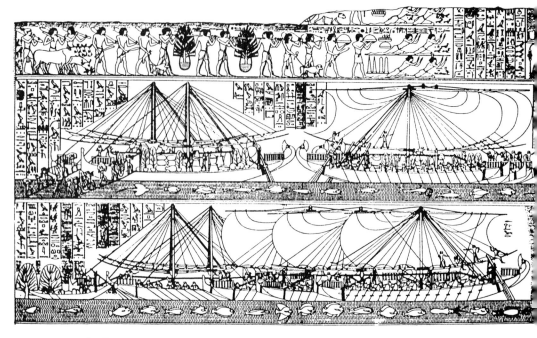

*The ships of Queen Hatshepsut, c. 1500 BC, arriving in Egypt from an expedition to the Spice Lands*

construction cost, methods. While the naval architects of the Renaissance could probably share a common language with their Egyptian, Phoenician and Greek predecessors, a present-day traditional shipwright would be completely bewildered in a modern industrial yard.

Our forefathers must have first ventured on inland waters, rivers and lakes, using natural floats such as the log, the reed raft, the clay jar, the inflated skin and the basket. The different possibilities were tested by time, and only the first two continued to develop. Maritime museums, especially in the eastern Mediterranean (Egypt, Greece, Israel), display the main types of local primitive craft, as depicted in ancient illustrations. Only rarely do we find their living descendants still in use, as in the case of the rafts of the lagoon of Oristano, Sardinia. With time, special kinds of boats were developed for river and open-sea voyages; these fell into two main types – long oared ships for coasting and battle, and round sailing ships for transport. This chapter will be concerned mainly with the latter.

The ancient Egyptians, who probably developed their craft on the Nile, ventured into the Mediterranean and Red Seas in the third millennium BC. It may be assumed that at this stage they were relying on the Semitic people of Syria and Lebanon to supply them with materials and probably also to build and man their boats, especially for long voyages abroad. (The employment of foreign labour was the usual practice with all the land-powers, such as the Assyrian Empire and the Hittites of Asia Minor.) Although the artistic representations are very detailed, and even some funerary models were found, we are left with more questions than answers as to the actual character of these boats and their seaworthiness, for these depended on their keel and fastenings, the working of the rigging and the steering devices, about which we have insufficient knowledge. The discrepancy between the historical data on the extent of Egyptian seafaring and the limited nature of the archaeological evidence has given rise to a surge of the imagination, fed by man's natural spirit of curiosity and adventure. Thor Heyerdahl, for instance, a native of the northern seafaring tradition, took up the challenge and proved the feasibility of oceanic crossings in elaborate rafts.

The link between these rafts and wooden seagoing vessels may be found in the sewn boats, wooden craft which were tied together by cord, then usually caulked for watertightness. This nail-less tradition was dominant in the Indian Ocean until the coming of the Portuguese, and is preserved to this day in a few examples on the East African coast. In the Mediterranean, this technique was replaced by the tenon-and-mortise joint at an early date, possibly by the Phoenicians. A wreck dating back to the second half of the sixth century BC, excavated at Bon Porté (near St Tropez in France), reveals a small boat that was assembled by cord going through holes in the planks, and fastened by small dowels driven into the holes, which served also to prevent the entry of water into the boat. Similar boats found in Yugoslavia (Nin) and Italy (Cervia, Pomposa) prove that this kind of boat continued to be employed in the Mediterranean, although on a limited scale, side by side with those based on more advanced techniques, well into the Middle Ages.

The famous Cheops ship found in 1954 beside the pyramid built by this Pharaoh is probably the oldest surviving ship yet found. Dating to about 2600 BC, it was a funerary barge, designed to carry the great monarch to his afterlife. It is over 40 m long, has no keel, and is built from short planks of acacia joined together like bricks. In 1988, a second ship was found next to it, and an interesting attempt has been made to study it without excavation and exposure. An air-tight hole was drilled, and a video camera lowered into the pit, equipped with a strobe light and ultra-violet filter and capable of

*Greek vase-painting depicting a merchant being pursued by a warship, c. 600 BC*

pivoting 180 degrees and rotating 360. The researchers were frustrated in their efforts to record the composition of the air trapped in the pit, but some first rate photographs were taken. The whole experiment constituted an important precedent for this type of probe, applicable to other sites with difficult access, such as caves and submarines.

In Crete and the Aegean Archipelago, another great seafaring tradition, parallel to the Egyptian one, had gradually emerged, reaching its height in Minoan and Mycenean thalassocracies. Again, our knowledge of these sea powers springs mainly from iconographic sources, such as seals and amulets, graffiti, reliefs and vase paintings, and from literary descriptions such as the epic voyages of the Argonauts and of Odysseus. These sources are so copious that the Belgian scholar Lucien Basch has been able to put together a veritable *'musée imaginaire de la marine antique'*. However, no actual remains of this period had been discovered. Historians were beginning to cast doubts as to the basic concepts of these so-called marine societies, when a striking discovery reaffirmed old theories and opened new debates.

In the marine scenes of the recently uncovered frescoes of Thera, a rich Aegean maritime tradition preceding the middle of the second millennium BC comes to life, depicted in vivid colours. This tradition seems to be characterized by a type of boat that is well suited to the short distances to be covered in Greek waters, and to the chronic state of piracy which existed there at the time. The crescent-shaped profile of these ships is rather slender and long (estimated at about 25 m) and actually double-ended, with a raised bow, decorated with flowers and other beautiful ornaments, and with an equally raised stern, ending in an awesome symbol – stylized horns or the head of a predatory bird or animal, a falcon or a lion. They are propelled by paddles and a single square sail, steered by a heavy oar at the quarters; there is a fin-like device designed to prevent drifting. Scholars are still arguing about the details of these ships' features, but after all, they are merely the view of yet another artist. The hard facts can come only from the ships themselves.

The greatest contribution of underwater archaeology is in the fields of naval architecture and harbour engineering. In the last generation, with tens of shipwrecks excavated and hundreds surveyed, our knowledge has been revolutionized. The Greek ship discovered in Kyrenia, Cyprus, is one of the first to be scientifically excavated, raised, preserved and reconstructed. The project was carried out by the Institute of Nautical Archaeology under the direction of Michael Katzev. Although it lay under 30 m of water for 2,300 years, almost 75 per cent of the hull was preserved. This made reconstruction possible, using the original wood carefully raised from the sea, treated with polyethelene glycol and finally reassembled. The American Richard Steffy, a great authority on ancient naval architecture who was in charge of the reconstruction job, admitted that he felt the contest of wits between himself and the ancient shipwrights. The ancient ship had been repaired many times during her long service at sea and was finally sunk by an act of piracy with at least four men on board, including the captain, whose belongings and arms were found among the remains of the cargo. The old ship is now on display in Kyrenia Castle, on the Turkish part of the island. Unhappy with this, the Hellenic Institute for the Preservation of Nautical Tradition undertook to build a living replica, with the scientific assistance of the original excavators.

The replica was launched in 1985, one of the most accurate reproductions ever completed, and is now sailing successfully under various scientific experimental programmes. She is about 15 m long and can carry a load of 30 tonnes. Her first voyage was from Piraeus (where she was built) to Kyrenia (where the original sank), recreating the route of the original ship's last voyage. Besides its scientific value, this voyage turned out to be a sweeping expression of Greek feelings concerning the present situation in Cyprus. On her second voyage, she was loaded with cargo, an equivalent of part of the original 400 amphorae and the many millstones which she would have carried as ballast. The captain of the replica is the son of the Cypriot fisherman-diver who discovered the ship in 1967. In the summer of 1986 she

*Roman mosaics from Ostia, the forum of the shipping corporations*

participated in the naval parade held in New York for the bicentennial celebrations of the USA.

Under present conditions, France is undoubtedly the leading Mediterranean country in the excavation of shipwrecks. Its shores are lined with ships sunk between the first century BC and the first century AD. The excavation of a Roman cargo ship off the Madrague de Giens near Cannes, at a depth of about 20 m, between 1972 and 1976, is a model of a systematic, multi-seasonal, underwater excavation, using all the new methods and tools available to modern research. An underwater museum has been planned, for the first time, to be built over the remains of this wreck. This is an impressive cargo vessel of about 300–400 net tonnage and a capacity of some 525–680 cubic metres. These facts were calculated on the basis of the 6,000 to 7,800 amphorae found on board, in three superimposed layers, each one weighing 50 kg when full of wine. It seems there was room for a fourth layer, which in this case was replaced by a cargo of smaller clay containers. Many of them still held their contents, a highly valued wine from Terracina in southern Italy, which had not improved after 2,000 years in salt water. On the other hand, a part of the hull under the cargo was very well preserved. Calculated to be about 30 m long, 9 m wide and 4.5 m deep, interesting features of what must have been a well-built ship were revealed: a strong keel, a concave stem serving as a cut-water and a massive mast-step. It had double planking and was protected against sea-worms with lead sheathing to the water line. The upper works and the rigging are missing, as is regretfully the case with most wrecks.

The sheer quantity of Roman wrecks off the French coast is indicative above all of the scope of maritime traffic between Rome and its western provinces, but it may also be the consequence of a practical fact; it is usually the cargo, in the form of many clay containers (amphorae), which preserves the hull buried under it and draws the hidden parts of the ship to the explorer's attention. Around the beginning of the Middle Ages, other forms of containers replaced the amphorae, such as *dolia* (huge clay containers, which usually broke up), and barrels (*botte*, tuns), which appeared first in the western Mediterranean. In the case of amphorae, the containers weighed as much as their contents, while the barrels were not only less brittle but weighed a tenth of their contents! In volume the amphorae are even less effective. The reasons for clinging to the amphorae despite their obvious disadvantages are difficult to trace, but are probably comparable to today's reluctance to accept plastic containers for choice wine. This mini-revolution in maritime packaging probably accounts in part for the scarcity of finds after

*Ancient stone anchors*

*Assumed origin of various types of stone anchors:*

(1) *Malta;* (2) *Beirut, with hierogliphic signs;* (3) *Lothal, India;* (4) *Byblos, Lebanon;* (5) *Pantelleria;* (6) *Crete;* (7) *Ugarit, Syria;* (8) *Kition, Cyprus;* (9) *Hala Sultan Tekke, Cyprus;* (10) *Motya, Sicily;* (11) *Swansea, England;* (12) *Pireus, Greece;* (13) *Agde, France;* (14) *Ambonne, France*

the classical period.

Anchors are another key find in the history of seafaring. Scattered all over the sea-bed, they have been raised and collected by fishermen and amateur divers. Many small boats still use to this day stone anchors which are sometimes reused old ones. Even in ancient times, the anchor had a high symbolic and ritual import, and was raised and reused in temples and tombs. Today it is still a collector's dream, from the stone weight to the admiralty anchor. The Roman period produced the most sophisticated anchor, a collapsible type made entirely of iron, which had disappeared by the end of that period not to reappear until the nineteenth century. But most ancient anchors were made of wood and lead, the stock being the main weight; later on the arms and shank formed the heavy part. There were many anchors of different sizes on board ship, for often they had to be abandoned. Even a stranded anchor may serve as an important tool for dating and locating seafaring activity, while *in situ* anchors are a possible indicator of the direction, size and type of the ship. Several scientists are engaged in cataloguing all those found in private gardens along the Mediterranean coasts, although being of uncertain provenance they lose most of their value.

After the classical period, then, wrecks are scarce and far apart, but the general trends of development may be traced. During the next thousand years, important changes were made in three interconnected parts of the ship: the hull, the steering and the rigging. These medieval ships are not fully known in detail but seem to be the shipwright's reaction to crucial global processes: the depletion of Mediterranean forests, the disintegration of the Roman Empire and its economic system, the Muslim conquest and the perennial war at sea which ensued, and the contacts with the Atlantic established at the end of this era. These changes raise the basic question of the nature of technological progress; they were doubtless, in the eyes of contemporaries, an unfortunate deviation from the good old traditions. In the case of naval architecture, the changes were more in the nature of adaptations and developments of features that already existed. These changes are the outcome of an innovative disposition and a spirit of receptivity which are at the base of all technological progress but which are not always associated with the Middle Ages.

The change in hull construction was probably the most decisive. The move was from the shell-first technique (by which the planking of the ship is first joined carefully by mortises and tenons, then reinforced by the inner frames) to the skeleton-first system (that is, the formation of the ship's keel, stem and stern, with all the frames, to which the planking is then nailed, and finished with caulking). This means that from being a carpenter's unique masterpiece,

53

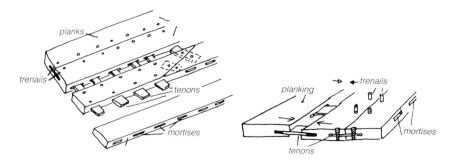

*The shell-first, mortise-and-tenon ship-building technique*

built 'by the eye', like the ships at Kyrenia and the Madrague de Giens, a ship could be built from a template, or designed on paper and mass produced by unskilled labour, supervised by the shipwright; this also saved raw material.

Two Byzantine wrecks of the fourth and seventh centuries, discovered off the Turkish coast at Yassi-Ada, and meticulously studied by Frederick van Doorninck of INA, brought to light this gradual move from one method of construction to the other, which reflected changes in the availability of raw materials and expert manpower, in the volume of trade and the costs of the shipping operation. Another wreck excavated by INA off Serçe Liman, also in Turkey, and dating back to the eleventh century AD, affirmed this trend: this bulky carrier was built completely on a pre-formed frame, but even at this date showed signs of an intermediate phase in the strange turn of the bilge, caused probably by lack of experience in shaping the frames properly and joining the top and bottom planks to fit.

The second major change was in the steering. All Mediterranean boats up to the thirteenth century were steered by two big oars set at the quarters close to the stern. At the end of that century, written sources mention the use of a Navaresque rudder on ships cruising in the eastern Mediterranean. This new stern rudder was developed in the Atlantic about a century earlier, and replaced the older type completely by the fifteenth century. The stern rudder facilitated the development of the transom stern, an important gun emplacement on board, and was thus connected to other crucial developments (see Chapter 10). It was considered by some scholars to be the key development which led to the ocean crossings and subsequent great discoveries in the New World, but this is highly disputed. There are even doubts as to the Atlantic origins of this kind of rudder, which had existed on Eastern (Indian Ocean) ships long before. Nevertheless, the stern-rudder seems to have penetrated the Mediterranean from the West, and its introduction, literary sources indicate, must have taken place on neutral ground, by people who had both a Mediterranean and an Atlantic coast – the French and the Spanish – in the Gulfs of Lion and Bayonne.

The third and most obvious change occurred in the ship's rig. The square latitudinal sail of antiquity gave way some time between the sixth and the ninth century to the fore-and-aft lateen sail, which disappeared again between the thirteenth and fifteenth centuries. As the reign of the lateen sail coincided almost perfectly with that of Muslim naval power, it was considered to be of Arab origin. Modern research has shown that Islam was probably merely the catalysing agent in the spread of this sailing system. It was especially suited to piratical raids and random shipping, which were indeed typical of the seventh to the eleventh centuries. Once conditions became better and ships larger, the square sail returned to be combined with the lateen into the beautiful rigging of early modern ships. When Columbus was preparing for his great voyage, he changed the rigging on two of the masts of his caravels *Nina* and *Pinta* from lateen to square sails, for they would do better in the Atlantic trade winds.

Also in the medieval period, there were close contacts with another great seafaring tradition, that of the Indian Ocean and China Sea. Here a puzzling enigma remains unanswered: why were these contacts so much less fruitful for the East, although people like the Egyptians, especially under the Fatimid Empire of the tenth to twelfth centuries, were active on both seas? Why did the East not incorporate the technical achievements of the West until after its collapse under the Portuguese onslaught? This enigma stresses the intimate connection of developments in naval architecture with the general economic, political and cultural background, and creates a challenge which can only be met by further research.

The fifteenth and sixteenth centuries are a watershed in naval architecture. From the sixteenth century on, there are scale models and accurate drawings, which radically changed the profession as well as our knowledge of it. In the first half of the sixteenth century, Vettor Fausto, a Venetian humanist and lecturer in Greek at the school of San Marco, carried out an important experiment. In a shipyard of the Venetian Arsenal which was placed at his disposal, he constructed galleys according to calculations based on the ancient Greek sources, and tested them in the basin of San Marco against the galleys of his time. His galleys proved to be 'of sound quality and speed, so that they are continually in demand, but are so durable that the Arsenal will make a great profit from them'. Nevertheless, there was opposition on the part of politicians resentful of change, and of master shipwrights opposed to the intellectual approach. Everybody was astonished at the man-of-letters who dirtied his hands in a practical activity. The humanists triumphed:

> Praise be to God that He has finally given ignorant men the chance to witness that men of letters know how to do more than just read and write. . . . No one can say any longer, 'keep away and stay with your writing desk and inkwells' (Concina, 'Humanism on the Sea)'.

From this period on, our interest in wrecks shifts from major constructional features to the ship-wreck as a time capsule. In fact, most wrecks of the later centuries have been dug outside the Mediterranean, for example the *Vasa* and the *Mary Rose*. The ships of this era were the ones to sail beyond the Straits of Gibraltar and make possible the exploration of the world. On the eve of the five hundredth anniversary of Columbus's rediscovery of America, we should remember that it was the Mediterranean seafaring tradition which made it possible.

The final blow to the Mediterranean ship-building industry came with the advent of steam and steel. During this development, iron and steel replaced wood much more quickly than steam replaced sails. Far into the twentieth century, there were sailing ships with metal hulls. The transition to steel hulls was dramatic and involved major adaptations, which shifted this industry from wood-rich to steel-rich centres, from investment in labour to financial investment. These new ships had a capacity of thousands of tonnes, compared with the few hundred of the average wooden ship.

With the latest move to supercarriers (some over 300,000 tonnes) and the great specialization in shipping (chemicals, oil, containers), many old, medium-sized but highly professional shipyards now spend their time in routine dock work, as the huge investments needed are beyond their resources. This is a source of frustration and pain for the governments and populations of countries which in the past enjoyed a leading role in the field.

While old centres of ship-building like Egypt and Lebanon, Greece and Turkey, Spain and Tunisia have renounced for the time being their respective historical roles in naval architecture, important developments are taking place in France and Italy. Since the imaginative dreams of Jules Verne, their pioneering efforts have mainly concentrated in the field of non-conventional craft, like hydrofoils and submarines. Some of the most advanced special-purpose submarines, both manned and unmanned, are

*Medieval Mediterranean cargo ships from the time of the Crusades and later:*
(a) *nef,* (b) *carrack*

being developed there now. One of these carried out the underwater photography of the newly discovered wreck of the *Titanic*. Experiments are being made with new submarines which avoid the use of nuclear power; it is hoped these will provide the answer to the most stringent ecological standards.

The industrial ship can never have the same place in people's hearts as did the ships of yore. Although the steel monsters still have proper names and are always feminine, people cannot love them and regard them as almost human. In the past, ships were decorated to protect them from evil, to impress their viewers and to accentuate their beauty, not just to keep the rust away. Ships' names are known even from ancient Egypt. They were usually the names of deities who were chosen to be the guardians of the ship and her voyage. The Greeks introduced names describing the ship itself – *Argo* (swift), *Charis* (grace) and the like. In Roman times, names like *Victory* (*Nike*) were common, along with the names of heroes and great men. Under difficult sailing conditions in the Middle Ages, many ships bore the names of two saints and more, just to be on the safe side.

The ritual launching of a ship with a ribbon and a bottle of champagne goes back to remotest antiquity. It started with an offering and a great feast, which were replaced by a coin set under the main mast, its worth reflecting the size of the ship. The blood of a sacrificial animal served to mark the ship's name. As life and daily bread were dependent on it, the ship became sacred. This was one of the reasons for the burial of ships, not so commonly found in the Mediterranean, though very prevalent in Scandinavia.

The ship gave endless inspiration to artists of all generations. They decorated the ship itself with figure-heads and elaborate picture-gallery sterns. After the introduction of the stern rudder, the aft attained large dimensions and was covered with decorations, to a point where it interfered with the functioning of the vessel. The French in the seventeenth century were leaders in this trend. Ships were the subject of endless expressions of yearning and devotion, shown by the votive offerings found in so many places of worship all around the sea. Ships that are long a thing of the past, with sails blowing (sometimes in different directions), still appear in popular drawings, and on coins and stamps. The wooden sailing ship, having passed its functional stage, lingers on, like other creative achievements of the past. It has become a motif of human culture, like a fish or a cross.

CHAPTER 5

# GATEWAYS AND HAVENS

THE DEVELOPMENT OF PORTS is one of the outstanding features of the relationship between man and sea in the Mediterranean. It is the expression of technical achievement, of adjustment to changing physical circumstances and economic conditions, of social and political cohesion. The biography of a port, like that of a ship, may tell us a great deal about the times.

The Mediterranean Sea, about 3,800 km from east to west, has a coastline of some 22,000 km, equivalent to more than half the circumference of the globe. Much of its shoreline is highly indented, and many islands stud its crowded waters. This has combined with intensive human activity over thousands of years, to give it the highest density of ports among all the world's seas. More than a thousand harbours are recorded along its coasts, most of them 30–40 km apart (a day's journey in the past). Obviously, the features of a port intended to give refuge to Minoan ships in the second millennium BC are different from those sought in an oil port at the end of the twentieth century. Consequently, only about 150 old sites still act as commercial harbours today, and just a third of these have been fully modernized.

The most ancient Mediterranean ports became defunct because of changes in the sea-level and other coastal processes (described in Chapter 1). When the sea started to rise, about 17,000 years ago, the ancient coastline was flooded; river mouths became inlets, easily navigable a long way inland. Most sites of that period are either below present sea-level, or located a few hundred metres inland. During the Bronze Age, about 5,000 years ago, conditions were finally stabilized, and the coastline reached its present configuration. In the eastern Mediterranean (as well as in the Iberian peninsula and elsewhere), river mouths silted up and wide sandy beaches formed.

By the late Bronze Age, Mediterranean river ports became rare, with a few famous exceptions (modern Seville, Arles, Cairo). Their remains are not architectural, but the visible results of the inhabitants' efforts to fight the

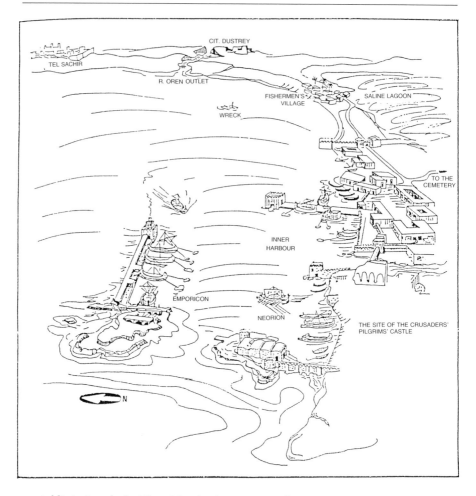

*Athlit in Israel, the Phoenician harbour* c. *seventh century BC*

changing physical conditions, in the form of river-diversions, dams and canals. Many pre-Hellenistic sites of western Anatolia – Miletos and Smyrna, Minoan Mallia in Crete, Canaanite Tel-Nami and Achziv in Israel – show man-made features designed to keep a silting harbour both free and protected. Actual port installations must have been minimal, but the wealth of imported wares found in these sites testifies to the intensive international maritime trade carried on.

The stabilization of natural conditions and the rise of new factors, such as the great thalassocracies which carried on an international maritime commerce and built up large navies for military expeditions, led to the foundation of the first coastal harbours, many of them still active today. Their reliance on natural features was still very strong, since the lack of significant tides in the Mediterranean has always made anchorage relatively difficult. These early harbours were located near an island or promontory, a natural bay, an inlet or a similar feature. But very sophisticated engineering was apparent right from the start; this may well have been passed inland in the form of improved construction techniques.

The main features of harbour engineering at the turn of the first millennium BC are present in the remains of two Phoenician ports dating to that era – Tabat-elHamman in Syria and Athlit in Israel. Most prominent are the headers (blocks of hewn stone laid with their narrow side out, perpendicular to the face of the wall), measuring an average of 0.5 × 0.5 × 2 m, which were designed to withstand the push of the waves and the pull of the currents. They were placed on a gravel foundation, to prevent the sea from undermining the whole structure. There are also flushing devices, in the form of spaces left in appropriate locations, occasionally provided with high sills, which prevented the sand and silt from entering the anchorage but allowed the free current in and out of the port and enabled the necessary drainage to take place.

Only major maritime cities and their chief colonies could afford this kind of harbour at the time. They became gateways opening from the sea to the land-masses behind, and the terminals of the great caravan routes leading to the sea. Other sites served only as havens for random anchorage and local trade along the coast. In many places, trade went on with the ships anchoring in the lee of islands and headlands, lighters setting up a kind of 'beach market' on shore, as described in this paragraph by Herodotus, which alludes to the Carthaginians (iv, 196):

They come and unload their cargo; then having laid it orderly along the beach they go aboard their ships and light a smoking fire. The people of the country see the smoke, and coming to the sea they lay down gold to pay for the cargo and withdraw away from the waters. Then the Carchedonians disembark and examine the gold; if it seems to them a fair price for their cargo, they take it and go their ways; but if not, they go aboard again and wait, and the people come back and add more gold, till the shipmen are satisfied. Herein neither party (it is said) defrauds the other; the Carchedonians do not lay hands on the gold till it matches

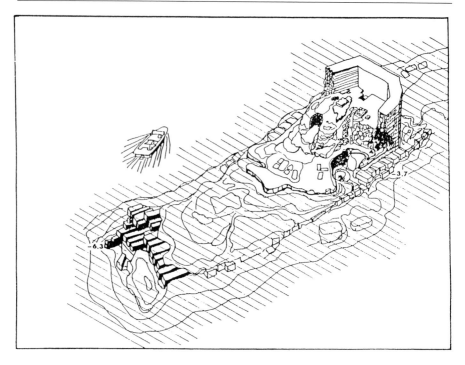

*The Tower of Flies at the entrance of the harbour in Acre, Israel: a view showing the structure above and below the sea*

the value of their cargo, nor do the people touch the cargo till the shipmen have taken the gold.

During the first millennium BC, the main components of the harbours were established. They were organized according to the *emporium* concept, which physically separated international exchange and local trade. The *emporium* consisted of a platform or a basin for loading and unloading operations, usually located in front of the port complex, either on an island, or by a separate breakwater. The connection to the port town was by tenders, and foreigners were not allowed in. Apart from the international and local commercial anchorages, there was usually a third basin, heavily guarded and sometimes dug inland, serving as the military harbour for the local navy.

Modern research has called this last type of anchorage a *cothon*, after its proper name in Carthage, the great Punic capital, in modern Tunis. The

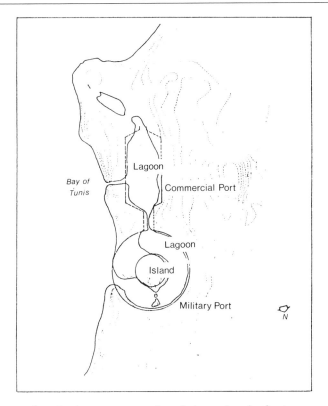

*Carthage, modern Tunis: a reconstruction of the ancient 'cothon'*

horseshoe-shaped inner harbour of Carthage is about 360 m in diameter. In its centre there is still a little island, where the fleet's leader used to live. A channel led to this harbour from the outer, commercial anchorage to the south of it. *Cothons* or inner harbours have been identified in several ancient port complexes, some of them erroneously, as in the case of Motya, the important Punic colony in the western coast of Sicily. The basin carefully dug and paved within the city walls, with a central groove and a channel connecting it to the sea, was previously thought to represent a *cothon par excellence*, but is now considered to be a medieval installation, probably a fish-pond.

Tyre (in Lebanon) was the most important Phoenician harbour in the Mediterranean and continued to be a major port throughout the ages. In the sixth century BC, the prophet Ezekiel described it with a mixture of hatred and admiration (27, 3–4): 'O thou that art situate at the entry of the sea, which art a merchant of the people for many isles . . . thou hast said, I am of perfect beauty. Thy borders are in the midst of the seas, thy builders have perfected thy beauty.' This was the site where, in the 1930s, the French archaeologist A. Poidebard pioneered underwater research into ancient harbours, using aerial photography and hard-hat divers. He identified the location of the northern and southern harbours and some details of the construction.

In the Greek world, engineering techniques were different from those used in the Phoenician orbit, and breakwaters were usually constructed as moles made of unhewn boulders, with regular masonry only on the top part, forming a quay. The functional division of the anchorage area into two or three parts was common, and the whole complex was usually closed and fortified, with a chain across the main harbour entrance. The Greeks called the complex *limen kleistos*, the closed harbour, a climax of their comprehensive architectural concept, incorporating the harbour within the port-city and offering solutions to problems of security and economics. Cnidos, Aegina, Syracuse and Marseille, to mention but a few striking examples, should first be seen from the sea, then visited with an eye to the city and harbour interface, represented by all the main features of a port complex: lighthouse and port entrance, sea gates, storage areas, public buildings, rectangular grid layout of the streets and quarters and the main street leading to the harbour. The politically-minded Greeks noticed the special mentality characteristic of the population of port-towns and concluded that 'maritime empire is the mother of democracy'. They meant it in a derogatory way, and recommended the separation of the port from the town, as in Athens and Piraeus, or Corinth and its ports, Lechaeum and Kenchreae.

A characteristic port feature became, in Hellenistic times, one of the seven wonders of the ancient world. It was the lighthouse of the great port of Alexandria, Egypt, built around 280 BC and named after the original island on which it was built – Pharos, which was connected to the mainland by the Heptastadion causeway. According to contemporary sources, it was 120 m high; this was in order that it could be seen also by day, as there is no high ground in the Delta. It was built in three main storeys and covered with shiny marble and bronze statues, while its beacon, fed by a perpetual fire and amplified by a sophisticated systems of mirrors, was said to be visible over 50 km away (modern lighthouses are visible from a distance of about 30 km). As Alexandria became the largest city in the Mediterranean, and its port the busiest and richest, the fame of its lighthouse spread far and wide, until its name became synonymous with the word for lighthouse in many languages. The Pharos fell apart gradually, until it was destroyed by a tidal wave after an earthquake in 1477, and later served as the foundation and building material for the fortress of Qait-Bay, guarding the entrance to the city's twin harbours. Another one of the great wonders of the ancient world was also a port feature – the Colossus of Rhodes, a huge statue at the entrance to the harbour, no remains of which exist today.

The Greek Naval base, the *neorion*, was characterized by the ship sheds, several of which were discovered in ancient Aegean ports. The most elaborate were naturally those of Athens, around the port of Zea. It is reckoned that there were 327 of them, each some 37 m by 6 m, roofed over in pairs, with columns in between. The trireme warships were hauled up mechanically on slanted stone slipways which extended into the sea. The wooden equipment (masts, yards, oars) was stored in racks over the boats, while another huge building housed the rest of the gear, such as sails and canvas, all neatly arranged in the two-storeyed aisles. The archaeological remains of these installations and the literary references to them provide much information both on the ships themselves and on the organization of the navy.

Under the Roman Empire, economic and political considerations dictated the construction of huge ports in places which were not endowed with suitable natural features. The Roman genius for engineering may have been best expressed in ports like Ostia, Leptis Magna and Caesarea Maritima, sites that astonish even the modern port builder. The Roman Vitruvius left us a few paragraphs on port building techniques in his monumental book on architecture (5: 12.2–7), while the Jew Josephus wrote a detailed description of Sebastos, the port of Caesarea Maritima, built by Herod the Great around 10 BC (*Jewish Antiquities* 15:330–342; *Jewish War*, 1:408–414):

> Notwithstanding the totally recalcitrant nature of the site, he [Herod] grappled with the difficulties so successfully, that the solidity of his masonry defied the sea, while its beauty was such as if no obstacle had existed. . . . What was especially notable about this construction was that he got no material suitable for so great a work from the place itself, but completed it with materials brought from outside at great expense. . . . Half of [the breakwater] was opposed to the surge of the waves. . . . The other half, supported on a stone wall, was divided at intervals by towers. . . . Into it had been built a series of vaulted recesses as shelters for sailors. And before them there was a wide quay which encircled the harbour and was a very pleasant place to walk around for those who wished to do so. . . . Below the city the underground passages and

sewers cost no less effort than the structures built above them. . . . Whenever the sea was driven in from offshore, it would flow through the whole city and flush it from below. . . . Now the city was completed in the space of twelve years, for the king did not slacken in the undertaking and he had sufficient means for the expenses.

These descriptions were either ignored or thought to be highly exaggerated until the advent of underwater archaeology. Archaeological work in ancient ports involves many difficulties; the chief of these is the fact that most ports of the classical period have continued their activities up to our own day. Later ports were usually developed on the same sites, which observed the original layout and made research both difficult and dangerous. But in some cases they became silted and dried up, thus allowing partial insights into their secrets. Aerial photography has become a valuable technique in the research of ancient ports, as have sonar surveys. However, full-scale research has had to wait for marine archaeology, which, except for a few pioneering efforts, has only recently turned to the study of ports. This has happened on a large scale with the work of CAHEP, the Caesarea Ancient Harbour Excavation Project. This project studies Mediterranean port towns as a chapter in the collective biography of the sea, a biography which cannot be based on the investigation of wrecks and cargo alone. Excavation at Caesarea has been connected with the planned construction of a power plant on the site. It was preceded by a submarine survey in 1960 and another archaeo-geological survey in 1975, and is becoming a revolutionary landmark in our understanding of harbour engineering and of Mediterranean marine economics in general. It draws many volunteers yearly from all over the world, to unravel the secrets of the site. The power plant has been built, and new extensions are planned, while the ancient harbour is still being excavated.

The excavation confirmed all the details of Josephus' description and added many surprises which he, not being an expert in this field, ignored or misunderstood. The main breakwater, running in a semi-circle from south-east to north-west, was found to extend more than 600 m into the sea, and is over 50 m wide at water-level. It was protected from the waves and spray by a light front breakwater, a device rarely used nowadays. Another, shorter breakwater, protected the harbour on its northern side. The area thus enclosed, constituting about 200,000 square metres, was divided into two basins, which contained small jetties to facilitate anchorage. In order to prevent the silting of the ports, there were sluice-gates with wooden hatches.

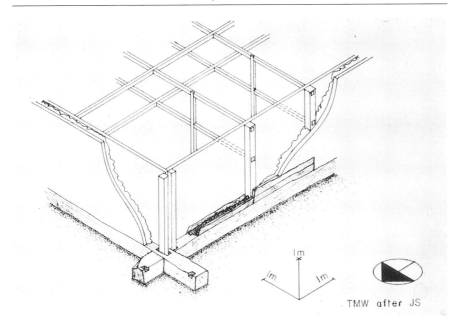

TMW after JS

*Caesarea, Israel: a reconstruction of the caisson technique of building the main breakwater*

There are also the remains of the two main entrance towers, and the entrance channel is easily discerned.

One of the most strikingly innovative features of this port is the method of its construction. At a depth of about 9–12 m, remains of wooden caissons, which served as the main building device for the breakwaters, were found *in situ*. These huge floorless, double-walled caissons, measuring 11.5 by 15.2 m, were built on land, then floated to their desired position. There they were submerged by filling the double walls with special mortar. After they had settled on the sea-floor, hydraulic concrete was poured into them. Much of this work was carried on by divers working underwater. It seems that in some places, the caissons were left empty, to be filled with sand by the sea itself. This whole process, unknown to Josephus, was described more than five centuries later in the work of Procopius, *De Aedificiis* (1.11.18–20). This author gives an account of the construction of two harbours in the Bosporus by Justinian I, the great Byzantine emperor of the middle sixth century.

In Caesarea as in any other great Roman port around the Mediterranean, the port city on land contained a customs house, store-rooms, places of worship and entertainment, baths and lodgings. A mariner or a traveller could disembark and find all his needs provided for. He must have felt it was indeed '*mare nostrum*'; he would be at home with the architecture, the public buildings, the street layout and the accommodation. Beyond the port area lay the local town – Levantine, Magrebine or Ponentine – but all around the Mediterranean the sea-front was Roman.

Caesarea was probably the first wholly artificial harbour in human history, built on a straight, wave-beaten stretch of coast. It was constructed by Herod, using techniques which later became standard in Roman port construction, as the main maritime centre of his little kingdom of Judea and it was to be its future capital city. What were his motives? Did he attain his goals? Why is Caesarea now in ruins? A harbour the size of Caesarea must have an economic *raison d'être*. In this case it was the transit trade of Far Eastern luxury items: these came to the Mediterranean and were then shipped on to Rome and to provincial centres, which were then developing consumption markets. These economic expectations turned sour after Herod's death, with the destruction caused by the crushing of the great revolt of 70 AD and the third-century recession in the empire at large. Natural catastrophe sealed the fate of this great harbour; archaeo-geological measurements have discerned two fault lines running parallel to the coast line, some 200 and 400 m west, which caused subsidence of 5–6 m, and Caesarea went into disuse rapidly, sinking with the unstable sea-bed on which it was built. Several Byzantine emperors tried to rebuild the deteriorating port, but to no avail. Finds from the third century AD on, such as ballast stones and amphorae sherds, were found on top of the sunken breakwater, indicating efforts to remedy the previous subsidence. Because it sank, the port was preserved, and now provides unique research possibilities.

Most port installations have to be in precise relationship to the water-level. As the Mediterranean has a relatively small tide and much of its coast is quite steep, this relationship is obvious and easily defined. Slipways and quays, mooring-stones and sluice gates, inner basins (*cothons*), channels, water tanks and the like are studied with special care in Caesarea as well as in Piraeus and Alexandria, Venice and Barcelona, and many other sites. They serve as a perfect indicator of changes in sea-level in historical times. Geologists usually lack the means of dealing with relatively recent and short spans of time, but Mediterranean conditions make this a possibility.

Fully developed Roman ports are up to the standard of ports today and, considering they were built without modern science and equipment, are indeed amazing. The mode of construction, which takes into account longshore currents, winter spray, river deposits, and the direction of infrequent winds, still has something to teach us today. Roman underwater techniques are not yet fully understood, but divers were certainly used for work on the construction. There is no doubt that there were certain sorts of lifting devices in use, such as cranes, but no material evidence of them has yet been found. The fact that some Roman harbours are sunk or silted now does not necessarily point to ignorance of the physical factors at play, but rather to the overwhelming importance of political and economic considerations. Without constant maintenance, even the best ports could not continue functioning. Once circumstances changed, nature was left to take its course, and the ports fell into oblivion.

Many classical ports fell victim to unavoidable natural processes, becoming either silted or submerged. Like Caesarea, Kenchreae in Greece and Pozzuoli in Italy were erected on unstable ground; they were preserved after submergence. Ephesos and Miletos, on the Aegean coast of Turkey, are striking examples of the opposite: they were completely silted up. The big and small Menderes rivers push the shoreline out 8–9 m each year, so that both towns are now far inland, with Ephesos some 15 km from the sea! The same thing happened to Rome's own port at Ostia, which can now be seen as a beautiful hexagonal formation adjacent to the Fiumicino airfield.

With the disintegration of the Mediterranean economic system at the fall of the Roman Empire, Mediterranean ports deteriorated rapidly. The Muslim period ushered in a further decline in maritime trade and coastal sites around the Mediterranean. During the eighth century, feudal Europe turned away from the sea, and the Abbasid Califs in Baghdad had an eastern orientation, with their maritime activity geared mainly to the Indian Ocean. The commercial revolution of the high Middle Ages and the parallel crusading movement breathed new life into the old ports. But it seems that the secrets of classical engineering were lost, or there was no economic incentive to invest as much in port installations.

Most medieval ports lacked mooring facilities, and it was quite common for trading vessels to lie at anchor while lighters linked them to the port. As a reflection of the nature of this period, emphasis was laid mainly on defensive features such as walls, towers and the ubiquitous chain at the harbour's entrance. Most instructive in both its similarity to and divergence from the old traditions is a description of the rebuilding of the port of Acre, about 50 km north of Caesarea, towards the end of the ninth century; this is preserved in the writings of the Muslim geographer alMaqdisi. According to him, the

SEA ELEVATION

governor Ibn Tulun summoned all the engineers and architects living along the coast to realize his project, but none of them knew how to build a structure underwater. Finally the author's grandfather, the architect Abu Bakr, was called from Jerusalem, and he carried out the work, using large beams of sycamore:

> These beams he set to float on the surface of the water, as a prolongation of the town walls [seawards], and he bound them one to the other; while towards the west he left the opening for a mighty gateway. And upon these beams he raised a structure with stones and cement. After every five courses he strengthened the same by setting in great columns. At length the beams became so weighted that they began to sink down; but this was little by little, and finally they rested on the sand. Then they ceased building for a whole year, that the construction might consolidate itself, after which, returning, they began to build . . . making a junction between this and the ancient city-walls . . . across the western gate of the port he built a bridge, and every night when the ships had come within the harbour they drew across the water-gate a chain, even as was the case at Tyre.

Many of the ports of this era stand almost intact today and have become

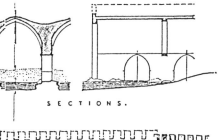

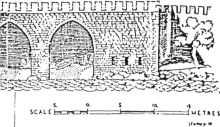

*The Tersena, the Seljuk Arsenal of Alania, Turkey, 1226*

popular tourist attractions – Aigues Mortes (Dead Waters) in France, Dubrovnik (Ragusa) in Yugoslavia, Rhodes in the Aegean. Their physical features – walls, towers, crowded merchant-dwellings, mosques, churches and monasteries – recreate the atmosphere of the times. These material remains are even more vividly brought to life by the many written and illustrated accounts of them which date from the crusading era – pilgrims' itineraries and accounts, heroic tales and poems, military plans and navigational instructions.

In Acre, people still live in five-storey thirteenth-century buildings built by the crusaders, and ships enter port in exactly the same way as Richard Coeur de Lion tried to do. Climbing the fortifications and roaming its caravenserais, the visitor can follow the charts drawn in the early fourteenth century. The exotic smells of the spices in its colourful market are reminiscent of Marco Polo, who was here on his way to the Far East. But its heyday lasted only briefly. With the Mamluk and Ottoman conquests it shrank to a small town, almost a fishing village. When maritime transportation in the Mediterranean picked up in the nineteenth century, it could no longer cope with the requirements of modern shipping, and lost its *raison d'être*. Like so many other historical ports in the Mediterranean, it is turning into a tourist marina.

One feature of port life which attained special importance in the medieval period was the shipyard, the Darsana or Arsenal (the words are a distortion of the Arabic *dar assina'a*). Here warships were built rather than stored as they had been in the ancient period. The Arsenal of Venice still occupies a vast area of the city. It was founded in 1104 and became the symbol of the economic and military power of the Venetian Republic. At the height of Venetian prosperity, the Arsenal employed 16,000 workmen. Their commotion was described by Dante in his *Inferno*:

> As in the Arsenal of the Venetians
>   Boils in the winter the tenacious pitch
>   To smear their unsound vessels o'er again,
> For sail they cannot, and instead thereof
>   One makes his vessel new, and one recaulks
>   The ribs of that which many a voyage has made;
> One hammers at the prow, one at the stern,
>   This one makes oars and that the cordage twists
>   Another mends the mainsail and the mizzen.

A less well-known but better preserved site is the Seljuk Arsenal of Alanya, along the southern coast of Turkey. Five arcaded halls stretch at the water's edge beneath the cliffs, guarded by a five-storey red brick octagonal watchtower, which bears an inscription dating the complex to 1225. In Spain, the magnificent Reales Atarazanas, the Royal Shipyards, accommodate the Maritime Museum of Barcelona and command attention in their own right; they are a well-preserved example of civilian Gothic.

   After the economic revival of the twelfth and thirteenth centuries, the great discoveries in the New World led to an even deeper decline in Mediterranean shipping activity, which reached its nadir in the eighteenth century. The opening of the Suez Canal in the nineteenth century and the growing reliance on oil in the twentieth introduced a new prosperity. But the old ports, with mountains at their back and their port area crowded with historic buildings, could not accommodate the big new ships and the volume of cargo without enormous investment. The ports that could not afford modernization turned their disadvantages to advantage with a flourishing tourist industry, or became chronically blocked, or both. Instanbul, the ancient Constantinople, capital of the Byzantine Empire for about a thousand years, is still struggling: although a modern oil and container port is developing at Hydarpasa on the Asian side, the water-front of the Golden Horn seems a hopeless bedlam, with a crowd of small boats going in all directions while huge ships sail in and out of the straits; civil and military, local and international, commercial and passenger traffic are all mingled in this historic waterway.

On the road to modernization, the ancient ports had to artificially create a deep basin for the new heavy steel and motor-powered ships, using the material from the dredging to reclaim new areas where the equipment needed for the handling of new kinds of cargo – cranes and warehouses – could be installed. Connections with the railway and super-highways were also critical. In many instances all this could not be done around the old ports in small bays, so completely new ports had to be constructed. This process emphasized the close relationship between port and boat. These complex technical, social and economic factors often pull in different directions: for the ship is above all mobile, while the port is static. Especially after the Second World War and the 'shipping revolution', ports became subordinated to shipping, mainly reacting to developments in ship design and function.

Marseille-Fos, a super-modern port complex, is the biggest in the Mediterranean today, a leading example of the evolution of an old port into one equipped for the twenty-first century. Its development required huge investment; it was designed as the ultimate in port technology. The excavations in the Bourse have revealed the long history of this port, from the first settlement by the Phocaeans, through its flourishing days as a Greek *polis* and Roman colony, to its heyday in the Middle Ages. The old ports received new functions; there are now specialized container facilities, roll-on, roll-off connections, oil terminals, and a whole new complex at Fos, connected by a canal to serve as the Europort du Sud. But the complex frequently lies idle due to stevedores' strikes and other problems, underlining the necessity for a suitable social and economic infrastructure as well as high technology.

These modern Mediterranean ports do not yet offer the efficiency of ports of the New World, but they have to a large extent lost the old Mediterranean port atmosphere. This evolved over many hundreds of years, as a result of the basic features of the coast – high mountains or deserts that stretch right up to the shoreline, which often made marine communications easier than overland routes. In a few places, especially on the islands, this way of life is still preserved. As the ferry is the most common connection with the mainland, life is centred around the harbour; people wait in the cafés and restaurants for its irregular arrival. There is no point in being impatient. As the weather is good most of the year, life goes on outdoors. In the evenings,

*A scale model to test wave impact on the breakwater in the port of Ashdod, Israel*

when the cool breeze blows from the sea, the whole town strolls up and down the water-front, socializing, showing off new clothes, and babies, exchanging political jokes. The evening promenade is still very much alive in many Mediterranean coastal towns; the most famous place for this is perhaps the Barcelona Ramblas. But in most large Mediterranean ports, this way of life is waning. Port time is expensive, and sailors who used to spend their spare time enjoying the amenities of the harbours are hardly allowed to go on shore. The action takes place in banks and offices, and the towns have become city conglomerates.

Modern Israel, situated at the historical crossroads between Asia, Africa and Europe, has a continuous history of over 3,000 years of port-building. Its land borders are closed for political reasons, and there is special emphasis on its outlets to the sea. Along its shores are ancient ports representing every important period in Mediterranean history, but none of these are adequate for today's needs. Under the British mandate, Haifa was built as the main modern harbour in the region and was destined to concentrate the industries which surrounded the end of the pipeline from Iraq. Under changing circumstances, the State of Israel built the port of Ashdod in the 1960s; this is situated about 100 km south of Caesarea. 20 years later, its turnover is surpassing that of Haifa and it is one of the fastest developing Mediterranean ports. Its planning, construction and further enlargement incorporate the latest developments in the field of harbour engineering.

The extensive reclamation works connected with the new Mediterranean harbours have initiated new directions for architectural and urban development. Given the general demographic growth and the even greater tendency of the population to concentrate along the coasts, future cities are planned which will be built in the sea itself; whether they are on reclaimed land or on artificial islands, these cities of the future are intended to provide an idyllic, pollution-free solution to population problems and could solve some of the problems of sea and city interface. In southern France, the coast is being reshaped according to various economic needs, and in Israel artists are creating political solutions by dreaming up huge reclaimed islands off the coast. In many other parts of the Mediterranean, scientists are developing models of new maritime urban centres, new cities in the sea.

CHAPTER 6

## THE GREAT EXCHANGE

T HERE IS STILL NO ALTERNATIVE, in terms of volume, weight or cost, to marine transportation. In earlier times, pack animals and carts compared very unfavourably; even today, in spite of the attractions of road, rail and air travel, transport by sea remains the best way to shift goods in bulk. To move goods by sea, no roads or tracks are necessary, only efficient ships and ports. For thousands of years, the three continents of Asia, Africa and Europe have used the Mediterranean to exchange goods and ideas.

The staple goods of maritime commerce at each period reflect the degree of co-operation and mutual dependence of the different parts of the system, the organization of shipping, the balance of payments, the standard of living – in short, the economics of the times. Today's staple in Mediterranean ports, as elsewhere, is oil. The rest is 'general cargo' – from machinery and electrical appliances to finished products and foodstuffs. What were the staples in bygone days?

The basic need of prehistoric man was good material for his tools. Obsidian, a black, glass-like stone of volcanic origin, is a rare material, found mainly on volcanic islands. When found on the mainland around these islands, it serves as an indicator of the extent of prehistoric seafaring. The earliest example so far was in the Franchti cave in the Greek Peloponnese, where obsidian from the island of Melos was found in a stratum dating from around 8000 BC. Prehistoric paintings, though many of them have been found in caves facing the sea, do not tell us anything about this stage of seafaring. We can only assume that these crossings were performed in the various primitive kinds of vessels described in Chapter 4. Another important centre of obsidian distribution was Lipari, the main island of the Aeolian archipelago to the north of Sicily. It seems the whole of southern Italy was dependent on the obsidian brought over by boat from that island, mainly in the Neolithic period. At that time, Lipari's importance far exceeded that of the fertile plains on the mainland. When stone tools were replaced by metal ones, Lipari revenged itself by preying on the boats carrying the metals. Later it became itself the victim of piracy, turning into the rugged desolate island it is today, where many of the inhabitants make their living by quarrying another kind of volcanic stone, pumice.

In the Bronze Age, the key raw materials to be carried by sea were copper and tin, the chief components of bronze. Cast into ingots, loaves and bars, they were shipped from mines all over the Mediterranean and beyond. The most common copper ingots were flat with four handles, the so-called oxhide type, while the tin ingots, much smaller, were usually flat on one side and convex on the other. Our information concerning the vast trade in metals underlying the great Bronze Age civilizations (Hittite and Egyptian, Minoan and Mycenean) derives mainly from literary and iconographic sources, for the metal objects found on land were either badly eroded or – more often – recycled and difficult to trace. However, two sensational finds of underwater archaeology have added considerable detail to the picture. They are two wrecks excavated off the southern Turkish coast, both more than 3,000 years old.

The first was discovered in the 1960s by a pioneering team headed by the Americans Peter Throckmorton and George Bass, near Cape Gelidonya, at a depth of about 30 m. The cargo consisted of 34 copper ingots averaging 20 kg apiece, inscribed with Cypriot signs and wrapped in matting. In between them were bits and pieces of broken ingots, a large amount of scrap metal, such as old knives, hoes and axes, scrap melted into small chunks, a few small, uniform ingots, probably used to serve as currency, and tin-foil. This floating smithy was equipped with balance pans and sixty different weights, made of deep-red haematite, to cover most of the eastern Mediterranean systems of measuring. There was a complete tool shop on board, from anvil and whetstone to hammers and swages for bending and shaping the metal. Only the furnace was missing, and this would probably have been erected on land. There was even a supply of clay for moulds, and the crew must have included an itinerant smith.

The second Bronze Age wreck was excavated twenty years later by the same group, off Kas, east of Cape Gelidonya. It is even earlier than the first and lies in deeper water. In addition to the copper and tin ingots, this wreck carried a varied cargo of precious materials; these included an exquisite gold goblet and Canaanite jewellery, high quality bronze tools and weapons, round glass ingots, unworked elephant and hippopotamus ivory, frankincense or myrrh, and other artifacts, which provided ample testimony to the high standards of this fourteenth-century BC golden age in the culture of the

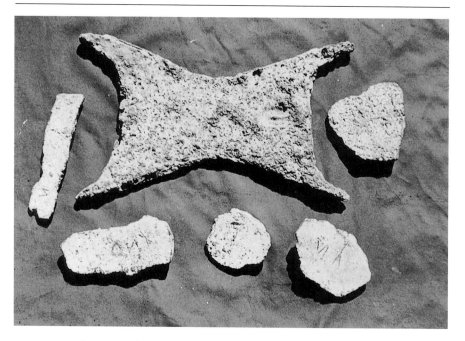

*Copper and tin ingots found as cargo of wrecked ships in the eastern Mediterranean*

eastern Mediterranean. Several other finds of ingots, in Crete and along the Syro-Palestinian coast, complement the picture. While copper ingots were rather large, tin was traded in loaves of 2–5 kg, and usually only used in thin sheets.

In the case of metals, the sources were so distant and the goods so heavy that, without transport by water, the Bronze Age could hardly have become so widespread. The Phoenicians, a Semitic people living along the north-eastern Mediterranean shore, soon monopolized the maritime trade in these raw materials, supplementing their international commerce in Eastern luxury goods. Tarshish means smelter in Phoenician, and the many places called by this name later, Tarsos, Tortosa and the like, point to the extent of this activity. The main copper mines were in Cyprus (from which derives the Greek name and the term used today) and Spain. The source of the tin is still controversial. Phoenician colonies like Cadiz, beyond the Straits of Gibraltar, point to Cornwall, England, which is indeed the only major source of tin within maritime reach of the Mediterranean region. The Phoenicians kept this tin route a grave secret, but its monopoly must have been challenged by inland sources, found in Iran and eastern Anatolia and even farther east in Asia. Tin constitutes only a small proportion of the copper alloy, which is over 90 per cent copper, so its transportation overland was feasible.

The world's oldest mining area still under production is RioTinto in Spain. It is 200 km north-west of Gibraltar and its present outlet to the sea is the Atlantic port of Huelva. Phoenicians, Greeks and Romans all left their mark there. The Rio Tinto company, now in charge of the mines, helps to finance a world archaeo-metallurgical centre based in London and headed by Beno Rothenberg, who became involved in this field during the excavation of the twelfth-century BC Timna Egyptian mines, north of Eilat, Israel. Besides the actual mining techniques (shafts, open galleries) and smelting methods (furnaces, moulds), mining was and still is beset with enormous problems of labour, fuel and transportation. In ancient times, the mines were a state monopoly, based on slave and forced labour. Fuel was provided solely by wood, hence the deforestation of entire regions around the mines. Transportation was by camel, mule and carts where possible, while for maritime traffic a new kind of round ship was developed, fit to carry the heavy cargo. The Rio Tinto mines in Spain are a living display of the modern solutions to ancient problems; curious types of trains and lifting devices are still *in situ*. It is intended to turn the whole place into a huge open-air museum, displaying all these different aspects of the mining industry in this one site where there has been 3,000 years of continuous activity.

In the classical world, with its great cities like Athens and Rome, the main concern of maritime commerce shifted to basic foodstuffs, and above all to the sacred trio of grain, wine and oil. Scholars have calculated that it would have been cheaper to move a cargo of grain from one end of the Mediterranean to the other than to move it 120 km on land, and the city of Rome in its heyday (the first and second centuries AD) was said to have consumed between a quarter and a half a million tonnes of grain a year! We know a great deal of the Roman grain supply, both from literary and iconographic sources and from archaeological finds. The main problems connected with the grain supply had to do with the Mediterranean climate and the nature of the grain. Grain is mobile and alive, in the sense that, in bulk, it flows like fluid with the movement of the ship, and if not kept cool and dry, it will deteriorate quickly and not last until the next harvest.

The grain was conveniently shipped during the summer, after its harvest in the spring and its transportation to the ports. The Alexandria–Rome grain line gave rise to the biggest ships in antiquity, some with a capacity of over 1,000 tonnes. The average grain ship was of 350–500 tonnes, an unexpected size affirmed by wrecks like those at Madrague de Giens and Albenga. Ships of this size seem to have disappeared from the Mediterranean for over a thousand years after the classical period, to reappear only in the late Renaissance. The hull of these ships was probably caulked on the inside with bitumen or resin or some other kind of sealing material, to which sheets of cloth were then attached, to prevent the moisture from spoiling the grain, which was transported in bulk or in sacks. The grain ships sailed in a convoy, the 'grain fleet', but even with the large ships specializing in this commodity, hundreds of other ships were busy carrying grain to Rome. The grain travelled with its *deigmata* – samples of the type and quality of the cargo – placed in small pots or leather wallets, and carefully sealed and labelled, to be handed over on arrival to guard against any fraud.

On arrival at its destination, the grain was stored in the great *horrea* (grain stores) around the harbours (Puteoli, Ostia) and in Rome itself, to be doled out to the population of the city or to be sold on the free market. These *horrea*, built usually of brick, have a typical feature: raised floors, designed to keep the grain from rotting. The loading and unloading of the grain cargoes were almost all done manually by porters, and were followed by transhipment up the Tiber, re-storage, marketing and distribution. A Roman citizen and his family used to get 5 *modii* of grain a month (1 *modius* = 6–7 kg), or about 1 kg a day, which makes for several hundreds of tonnes a day just for the Roman population registered by the grain officers, some 200,000 families.

The organization involved with the grain supply was enormous – state agents (*frumentarii*), private merchants (*negotiatores*, *mercatores*), shippers (*navicularii*), porters (*saccarii*), etc. Some time in the middle of the first century, it started developing from a private enterprise into a system partly controlled by the state. The *cura annonae* was considered an essential part of good government, for 'if it is neglected, the utter ruin of the state will follow', in the words of the Emperor Tiberius in 22 AD. Fifty years later, according to the historian Josephus, Africa fed Rome for two-thirds of the year, while Egypt took care of the last third. As Rome and the other big centres of consumption increasingly depended on the timely arrival of the grain from the colonies and provinces, the grain supply became a major political issue. A threat to the complex system could, and often did, disrupt life and government.

The wine jar could serve as the emblem of underwater archaeology. Many thousands of them have been found, sometimes with their contents intact, on the sea-bottom. In many cases, they preserve the hull of the ship underneath. A ship in antiquity was marked 'of a thousand amphorae' in the same way that we speak today of tonnes (tun, a wine barrel). In the case of these ancient containers, it is not wise to go by the dictum 'Look not at the jar, but at what is contained therein' (Fathers 4:20). The jars in themselves are of great interest, besides their aesthetic value. They often carry their own identity cards, in the shape of their handles, necks and lips, and in the stamps and inscriptions on them. These tell us many stories of their provenance, destination, and of the quality of their contents. After use, the jars could not be refilled. They served for storage in private houses, their bigger sherds were used for tiles and pipes, sometimes as writing material, and the smaller ones to pave the Roman road system, and as a scratching implement (Job 2:8). In Rome today there is an artificial mound made of the jars discarded in antiquity, the Monte Testaccio. By the amount of whole and broken amphorae found, one might come to the conclusion that drunkenness was the cause of the fall of the Roman Empire.

The Roman wine trade was a risky but very rewarding business. Both aspects are evident in the story of Trimalchio, the archetype of the rude *nouveau riche*:

> I conceived a passion for business. I will not keep you a moment – I built five ships, got a cargo of wine – which was worth its weight in gold at the time – and sent them to Rome. You may think it was a put-up job; everyone was wrecked, truth and no fairy-tales. Neptune gulped down thirty million in one day. Do you think I lost heart? Lord! No, I no more tasted my loss than if nothing had happened. I built some more, bigger, better and more expensive, so that no one could say I was not a brave man. You know, a huge ship has a certain security about her. I got another cargo of wine, bacon, beans, perfumes, and slaves. Fortunata did a noble thing at that time: she sold all her jewellery and all her clothes, and put a hundred gold pieces into my hand. They were the leaven of my fortune. What God wishes soon happens. I made a clear ten million on one voyage. I at once bought up all the estates which had belonged to my patron. . . . When I came to have more than the whole revenues of my own country, I threw up the game; I retired from active work and began to finance freedmen (Petronius, *Satyricon*, 76).

The amphorae were treated on the inside against the loss of fluids, with caulking materials such as resin, wax, pitch or bitumen, or by immersion in a limey solution. The Canaanite jar was probably the first to be intentionally adapted for sea voyages, some time in the second millennium BC. They

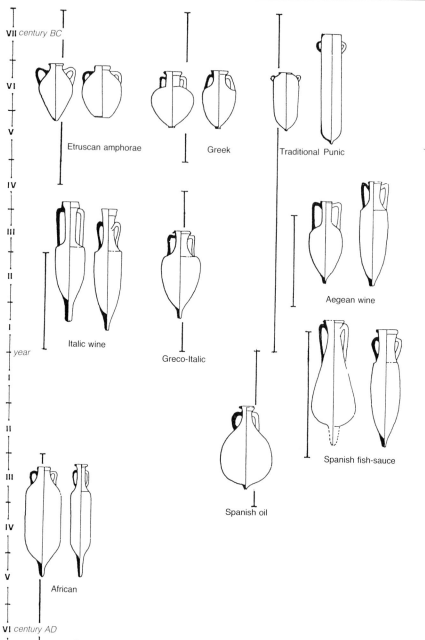

VII *century BC*

VI

V

Etruscan amphorae

Greek

Traditional Punic

IV

III

II

Italic wine

Greco-Italic

Aegean wine

*year*

I

II

Spanish fish-sauce

III

IV

Spanish oil

V

African

VI *century AD*

*Clay containers used in maritime transportation, mainly for wine and oil*

gradually developed the typical massive ear handles and the conical shape so well-known from museums and underwater sites all over the Mediterranean. An average amphora held just over 25 litres of wine, while the wholesale trade also used *dolia* (singular, *dolium*, which contained 525 litres and was equal to 20 amphorae). These huge containers usually stayed put, either in the cellars or on board ship, and the wine was transferred from them to the normal, portable jars. As already mentioned, the amphora weighed as much as its contents, while the barrel weighed only 10 per cent thereof, and was far less brittle. The stoppers were usually made of unbaked clay; these have been found on land with marks of cloth or vine leaves on them, which prevented contact between the contents of the jar and the stopper. There were also baked clay stoppers, held in place by cord, as well as stoppers made of limestone, bone, wood and finally cork. A large number of the stoppers were marked by different signs. In many cases, the jars on board were stored in layers, with the upper row carefully arranged on the row below. Some jars were found with a hole drilled near their base, probably revealing the antiquity of the practice of stealing wine on board.

Vines grow in most Mediterranean countries, so export wine relied on its special quality. The ancients used herbs, nuts, various resins and other materials to improve the taste of their wines and help preserve them longer. The wine was frequently quite concentrated and was used diluted with water. In order to maintain their reputation, the different centres used to control the quality of the exported wine. This is the reason for the elaborate system of handle marks, known especially from Rhodes, Thasos, Samos and Naxos (the main centre for the cult of Dionysos). The western provinces, like Gallia and Iberia, started to grow vines after the Roman conquest. Before that time, the people probably drank beer. The Emperor Domitian (AD 81–96) tried to fight this competition by destroying the vineyards in France and Spain, but later the wine trade became open to all. The wine merchants in the provinces turned into an important factor in the economy, contributing to the empire's instability in the third and fourth centuries. The fall of Rome and the conquests of Islam, which prohibited the drinking of wine by its followers, almost destroyed this industry. Only in the late Middle Ages did the export of wine start to regain its ancient place in maritime commerce.

Today the Mediterranean has long lost its monopoly in the wine industry. Countries and regions bordering on it, like northern France and Portugal, became great producers. Mediterranean wine experts planted vineyards in the New World, in South Africa and Australia. Nevertheless, until the middle of our century, 80 per cent of the world's wines came from Mediterranean

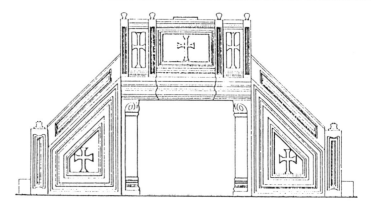

*A model of the ambo for a pre-fabricated Byzantine church interior of the sixth century AD reconstructed from its marble components discovered off Marzamemi, Sicily*

countries. In 1974, which was a peak year in wine production, Mediterranean countries produced over 228,040,000 hectolitres of wine, about 25 million tonnes. Wine production today constitutes a stumbling block to the EEC economic policy. France, for instance, is jealous of its competitors in Italy, Spain and other countries who are trying to move into the European and world markets.

The olive, because of its high oil content and good preservation qualities, was in antiquity a very important concentrated food, particularly useful for periods of scarcity and long voyages on land and sea. It was first cultivated in the Middle East, where it became the symbol of peace and affluence. Olive oil, beside providing nourishment, was used as fuel in the beautiful clay lamps which have been found in all Mediterranean countries in the past. It was highly prized also in medicine, cosmetics and for ritual uses. Twice as expensive as wine, it was shipped in easily identifiable jars, smaller than those used for wine and made of a better quality clay. Even after the introduction of the barrel, clay jars continued in use for oil, until in modern times glass and metal containers replaced them.

To this day, the olive groves are a distinct feature of the Mediterranean landscape. In Spain, which produces over 30 per cent of the world's olives and olive oil, more than 30,000 square kilometres are planted with olive trees. Most olive growing countries outside the Mediterranean do not produce olive oil, so Mediterranean countries still provide over 90 per cent of the

*Bodrum, Turkey: a reconstruction of an eleventh-century shipwreck from Serçe Liman*

*A traditional shipyard in the village of Kilada, Greece*

*Ephesus, Turkey: the road leading to the silted harbour, now about a mile inland*

*An aerial view of the sunken harbour at Caesarea, Israel*

*Genoa, Italy: the old harbour at the height of its activity*

*Genoa: the modern harbour is the busiest in Italy*

*Mazara del Vallo: the ancient harbour has become one of the most important fishing ports in Italy*

*Hydra, Greece, a typical old Mediterranean small port*

*Pumice in Lipari*

*The grain stores (*horrea*) in Ostia*

*The Grand Bazaar of Istanbul: for hundreds of years this was a main transit point for oriental spices and textiles*

*A votive painting from Malta. It was painted during the Second World War as a thanksgiving for safely surviving the aerial attack on the battleship HMS* Warspite *off southern Italy*

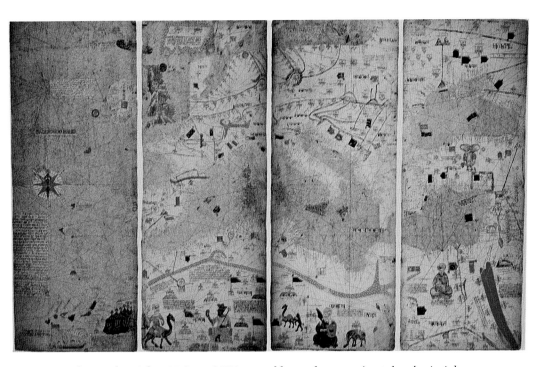

*The Catalan Atlas, Majorca 1375: a world map drawn on 'portolano' principles*

*Palermo, Sicily: a forest of masts in a modern marina*

world's olive oil. Countries like Italy, Greece and Israel are developing modern mechanical ways of gathering the olives, using a hormone treatment designed to facilitate the disconnection of the fruit from the tree.

Besides these staples, maritime commerce in the classical world dealt with heavy portables, like millstones, that were also used as ballast. Trade in, and pillage of, antique sculpture was widespread even in classical times, and sea transport was the best means of carrying it out. The first underwater excavations were inspired by a chance find made in 1900 off the island of Antikythera in the Aegean, which consisted of a Roman wreck full of looted Greek treasure. Near Riace, Italy, two life-size bronze statues were discovered in 1972, complete with inlaid eyes and traces of paint, exquisite specimens of fifth-century BC Greek art. Architectural elements – columns and capitals, sarcophagi and burial stones – are scattered all over the Mediterranean sea-bed. In Marzememi, south-eastern Sicily, the marble and porphyry parts of the interior decoration of a sixth-century church were found under water, including columns and slabs of the altar, canopy and pulpit. This pre-fabricated church, to be finished in local materials, was probably destined for North Africa. It must have been connected with the mission of Justinian I, the great Byzantine emperor who reunified the Roman Empire, using Christianity as a binding force.

In the early Middle Ages, the Mediterranean economy reverted to pre-classical times. Apart from raw materials (such as timber and iron) and slaves, which were shipped from the barbarian West to the civilized Muslim East, maritime commerce dealt mainly in luxuries, as in the days of King Solomon and the Queen of Sheba. Most of these luxuries came from the Far East, passing through many hands during their long transit journey. The risks along the way are hard to imagine today, but the profit to be had was manifold. Minority groups like Syrians and Jews ventured into this precarious business. The Jews were probably the only ones who would carry wares the whole distance to their destination, as in the rare mid-ninth-century description by the Muslim scholar Ibn Khordadhbeh:

These merchants speak Arabic, Persian, Roman, Frankish, Spanish and Slavonic. They travel from the East to the West and from the West to the East by land as well as by sea. They bring from the West eunuchs, slave girls, boys, brocade, beaver skins, marten furs and other varieties of fur, and swords. They embark in the land of the Franks on the Western Sea, and they sail toward alFarama [Pelusium]. There they load their merchandise on the backs of camels and proceed by land to alQulzum

[Suez], twenty five parasangs distant. They embark on the Eastern Sea and proceed from alQulzum to alJar and to Jidda [the ports of Medina and Mecca, respectively], then they go to Sind, Hind, and China. On their return from China they load musk, aloe wood, camphor, cinnamon and other products of the eastern countries and they come back. . . . Some of them sail for Constantinople in order to sell their merchandise to the Romans. Others proceed to the residence of the king of the Franks to dispose of their articles.

Spices were used in food preservation, medicine, cosmetics and dyeing. The most famous medieval merchant manual, *La pratica della mercatura*, written by the Tuscan Francesco di Balduccio Pegolotti between 1301 and 1340, has preserved a list of 288 'spices' and their uses. He marks with a dot the 'minute spices', those seasonings and aromatics which were sold in small quantities and for high prices. No gourmet shop, oriental boutique or health food store today would offer such a variety. A prominent place in this kind of manual was held by the fancy oriental textiles, from Chinese silks to Turkish draperies, including Indian cottons, Mesopotamian *moselins* and *tuffetas*, Damascene *brocards* and Armenian camel's hair rugs. These exotic fabrics became common among the upper classes in the growing European towns and helped to develop the rising European textile industry.

During these centuries, when the East had complete economic superiority over the West, its own resources in basic raw materials like timber and iron were being depleted. This happened gradually through the classical period, after centuries both of intensive maritime war and trade and of a high standard of living which had involved heated baths and energy devouring industries like metal work and textile dyeing. After the sixth century, the forests of Lebanon and southern Anatolia, of Cyprus and Sicily and of North Africa were not producing enough timber suitable for ship construction, monumental building and war machines. Syria and Tunisia joined Egypt, a country which had always depended on import, in their quest for timber. The Frenchman Maurice Lombard has tried to explain the Muslim expansion west and north, as well as certain Byzantine counter-moves, as a direct consequence of this quest. In any case, the shipping of timber and iron across the Mediterranean in the Middle Ages assumed unequalled economic and political significance. During the crusading era this trade was repeatedly banned by the Church under threats of heavy fines and anathema, but the very repetition of the ban proves the continuity of the trade.

After a long period during which international trade was a hazardous business left to the Jews and other adventurers, the Italians came to control Mediterranean maritime trade. The Venetian *muda* (sailing system) and the Genoese maritime routes, as well as the activity of other maritime centres such as Aragon and Provence, created the infrastructure for the success of the three Cs – Commerce, Crusade and Culture. In the fifteenth century, even before the great discoveries in the New World, the Islamic world was losing its economic superiority over the West, as the economic historian Eliyahu Ashtor has demonstrated: its manufacturing techniques became archaic, and the demand for its high-quality finished goods dropped as the West gradually provided its own cheaper versions of products which were formerly the mainstay of the eastern export trade, such as sugar and paper, woollen materials and later mechanical equipment. The Ottoman conquest in the sixteenth century brought to the East a short period of prosperity, followed by a steep decline which lasted well into the twentieth century.

After lying dormant for several centuries, the East has compensated for the technical and industrial superiority of the West with its mineral oil. The dependence of the developed countries of the north-western shores of the Mediterranean on oil pumped in the developing countries to their south-east has created a novel economic situation, a new balance of payments, and modern forms of exchange. The position of Libya and its complex relations with Italy, for instance, are reminiscent of the days when it served as the granary of Rome. As a natural resource, oil cannot benefit the entire economy of its countries of origin in the way the export of finished goods would do, but even with this basic limitation, its expected impact on the national economy of the countries involved has not yet realized its potential. Even the transportation of the oil is carried out largely by tankers belonging to other countries.

In this oil era, the Mediterranean Sea has grave problems of its own. Serving as a main thoroughfare for the transit of oil, the Mediterranean, with less than 1 per cent of the surface of the world's oceans, carries over 35 per cent of its oil transportation, that is over 350 million tonnes a year (1981), including the output of local wells. It is primarily a feed line to some of the world's most industrialized nations lying to its north, which consume about three-quarters of the total amount of oil transported across the Mediterranean; another quarter moves on into the Atlantic and to other destinations.

This enormous demand for oil started after the Second World War. Since then, there have been many fluctuations, which have deeply affected the whole region. Since the nationalization of the Suez Canal in 1956, the route from the Persian Gulf around Africa, with Rotterdam as the terminal and

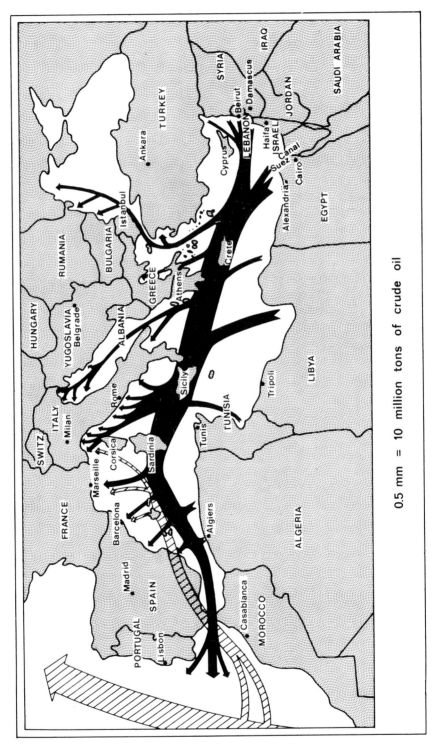

0.5 mm = 10 million tons of crude oil

*Oil flow in the Mediterranean*

distribution centre, has gathered momentum. The Arab–Israeli wars and the blocking of the Suez Canal between 1967 and 1975 had two main effects – the reinforcement of the Cape route and the development of alternative pipelines. The great demand for oil in the late 1970s drove Egypt to act on two apparently contradictory projects: increasing the capacity of the Suez Canal in both width and depth, for ships of 150,000 DWT (deadweight tonnes) instead of the 60,000 DWT it could accommodate before, and laying the SuMed Pipeline parallel with the canal, for a distance of 320 km; in the 1980s this transported as much oil as the Suez Canal and sometimes twice as much. The Lebanon crisis and the Iraq–Iran war drove the old Syro-Lebanese pipelines out of business, but both Israel and Turkey have constructed new pipelines, from Eilat to Ascalon in the south, and to the bay of Alexandretta in the north. Notwithstanding all these costly solutions, half the oil consumption of southern Europe still arrives through the Straits of Gibraltar!

The trends in the 1980s have been a general, though not constant, drop in oil prices, a decline in the oil production of the established centres (i.e. the North African countries), the rise of new ones (such as Egypt) and the discovery of new wells off the coasts of Greece, Italy and Spain. The developed countries are shifting to other sources of energy, with France, in the lead, hoping to rely on nuclear energy for 70 per cent of her total requirements in the 1990s. The oil-producing countries, realizing their 'time of grace' is running out, will concentrate in the future on the general development of their economy, rather than on the export of oil as raw material. The take-off phase is over, and now is the time to assess the progress made and ensure that it becomes irreversible.

Oil transportation has revolutionized shipping in general. The super-tankers developed for this purpose drove the older types of carrier out and made special arrangements in ports and docks necessary. Pipes laid across land and on the sea bottom are in turn challenging the supercarriers. The TransMed line between Algeria and Italy, including 180 km laid underwater at a depth of 700 m, carries more than 12 billion cubic metres of LNG (liquified natural gas) a year, and is an admirable feat of engineering. The next step would probably be a similar pipe from Oran in Algeria to Cartagena in Spain. The introduction of each of these methods causes a chain reaction in the whole shipping world.

Another major factor in modern maritime traffic is containerization. In the past, changes in packaging material deeply influenced the system of transport, as when barrels replaced jars. Recently, the containerization of general cargo altered the nature and rhythm of maritime traffic. Together with the roll-on, roll-off system, it necessitated profound changes in ships, ports, financial and commercial organization, the labour force – in short, it revolutionized maritime transportation. Containerization has substantially increased the mobility of cargoes, reduced handling costs, and provided better protection and security for the cargoes themselves. On the other hand, it concentrated traffic in a few major points, and made a dependent network of transhipment by feeder lines to other minor points necessary. This arrangement is particularly suitable to the Mediterranean, where Malta, for instance, is responding to the modern trend by building a new container terminal at Marsaxlokk.

Maritime transportation is notorious as one of the most sensitive sectors of the world economy. In addition to its own inherent fluctuations, it reflects any agitation in other sectors of the economy, even those which are only indirectly related to it. At the beginning of the 1990s, the world shipping industry in general, and Mediterranean shipping in particular, is in a critical phase, which will hopefully be transitory. There is a considerable overcapacity; there is a protracted imbalance between supply and demand. Competition is fierce, and developing countries find it increasingly difficult to make their way into the field. At Piraeus, dozens of ships rot in the harbour, the ghosts of one of the world's largest merchant fleets. The importance previously attached to freight rates, which even the experts admit to be more a matter of art than of science, is shifting to different issues such as the connection with other lines, with land transportation, with the market and with investors.

At the end of the twentieth century, the Mediterranean is an inseparable part of the world's system of maritime transportation. Only a small percentage of the goods carried across it will be exchanged internally; most of its traffic consists of international exchange between the Mediterranean countries and other markets around the world's oceans.

In addition to oil, the developing Mediterranean countries are specializing in subtropical agricultural produce, like citrus fruit, and an assortment of vegetables. During centuries of Muslim imperial rule, Mediterranean lands were enriched by many agricultural products and innovations. These products, improved by modern scientific methods, are an important item of export to the EEC. With nuclear energy and the rapid industrialization of countries south and east of the Mediterranean, what will be its staple goods of the future? Hopefully, future staples will express a dynamic, prosperous economic system, that will unite all the countries around the Mediterranean for their common benefit.

CHAPTER 7

# STEERING TO THE HORIZON

WHO DISCOVERED AMERICA AND WHEN? This question can no
longer be phrased in such simplistic terms: modern science has
shown the answer to be much more complicated and intriguing than was
previously thought. Pre-Columbian contacts are now pushed back several
millennia to prehistoric times, and many factors and situations over the
succeeding millennia are pointed out as possible forerunners of the important
event. The protagonists of the different theories do not lack evidence to
prove their point – and if it is lacking, they sometimes create it. The subject
has always been a matter of national pride. Now, as we approach the five-
hundredth anniversary of Columbus's voyage, debate is as heated as ever.
The Spanish and Portuguese cling of course to the obvious discovery at the
end of the fifteenth century, planned and financed by them; the Italians
stress the seafaring traditions of Columbus and his company; the Scandina-
vians have found material evidence of the stories of their sagas, which tell of
mysterious lands in the West; some historians of the ancient Near East are
positive about Phoenician influences in the western hemisphere, while
neutral parties insist that there were sporadic contacts from time immemorial. Today, we could put the question thus: of what nature were the cross-
Atlantic contacts in the different periods and what was their impact on both
sides of the ocean? The important fact is that Mediterranean seafaring was
technically and mentally ripe for the great discoveries at many points in the
past: during the heyday of Phoenician and Greek activity in the first
millennium BC; at the apex of the medieval commercial revolution of the
thirteenth century, maybe even in Egyptian and Minoan times. When the
voyages of discovery finally took place, there was no way back and the world
changed drastically. For thousands of years experience had accumulated in
the inner sea, in preparation for this breakthrough.

The Mediterranean is highly suitable for the beginnings of navigation
without instruments. Latitude was defined by astronomical observations,

longitude by the shape of the sea, long and narrow, stretching east-west. The many inner seas are well-defined geographical entities, marked by straits and capes. Almost all of the many islands may be seen from other islands or from the mainland, and serve as useful stepping-stones. There are no major currents of great magnitude. Last but most importantly, sea transportation is often more practical than moving on land, even for short distances, as land routes around the Mediterranean are often blocked by mountains and deserts reaching to the coast. No wonder that it was in these waters that man ventured out into the open, beyond known coasts.

The Mediterranean weather was a decisive factor in the development of navigation. This weather system is caused by the fact that the region is a passageway, even in the barometric sense, between the subtropical area in the south and the Euro-Asian block in the north. In the winter, barometric pressures in the north are much higher than those over the sea, with two typical depressions around Genoa and Cyprus. Cold air masses penetrate the warmer Mediterranean basin, and cause instability, strong winds and precipitation. In the summer, when northern air masses are prevented from affecting the system, the local pressure zone creates a stable situation, with high temperatures and lack of precipitation. Rain falls mainly during six months of the year, with a rise in precipitation from south to north and from east to west, so that the north-western regions get much more rain than the south-eastern ones. The months from May to October are almost completely dry, with clear skies, in most regions. These clear skies helped the early development of astronomical observations as aids to navigation.

The continuous mountain ranges almost all around the sea, the vast desert areas on its south and east, and the complex shoreline topography of much of the coast, consisting of many inlets and islands, create conditions which give rise to several regional and local winds. The most prevalent are the winds blowing from the north-west, which are most pronounced in the Aegean, where they were given their name Meltemi or Etesian (etesian means periodical). These winds made sailing in the Mediterranean possible up to the steam era; the passage eastward was quite effortless; from east to west, boats had to win their way against the wind. The Scirocco is the Italian distortion of the Arabic word *sharq*, meaning east, and is the hot and dry wind blowing from the south or south-east. In Arabic this wind is called Khamsin, or 'fifty', as it is believed that there are some 50 days during the year in which it blows. In the Magreb, this same wind is called Chili; in Libya, Ghibli; and in Spain, Leveche. It is most prevalent in the spring and autumn, and helped mariners to go west. The Mistral is a dry and cold wind, which in the winter penetrates the Mediterranean from the north, through mountain gorges and river streams. Its force is augmented by the 'tunnel effect', so it can reach 150 km per hour. It usually blows for a few days, at about 35 km per hour, and is mainly directed at the coasts of Spain and France. A similar wind is the Bora, affecting the northern Adriatic and the Aegean. In Yugoslavia they say 'The Bora is born in Senj, married in Rijeka and dies in Trieste.' This dictum, although it does not reflect the wind direction, grades its force faithfully. There is a north-easterly wind which is also cold and dry, called Gregale in Greece and Italy, Sharkiyeh in the eastern Mediterranean countries, and Levanter in Spain. Finally, the westerlies in the western Mediterranean are called Libeccio in Italy and Vendaval in Spain. In the medieval Mediterranean charts (see p. 000), most of the wind-rose markings are derived from these winds: Tramontana (N), Greco (NE), Levante (E), Syroco (SE), Ostro (S), Garbino (SW), Ponente (W), Maestro (NW).

To the ancient Greeks, this encircled sea was *thalassa*, the great open sea, in contrast with the inner basins which they named *Pelagos*. Even the Mediterranean can become vicious at times, and usually does so without any warning. Mediterranean storms cannot be compared in scale to oceanic ones, but the weather is unstable and the changes usually come as a surprise. Here there are no trade winds, monsoons and the like; the many straits and capes fix the routes, which are often quite dangerous. The currents in the Strait of Messina in Italy, or around Cape Malea in Greece, are to be reckoned with even by modern craft. In this respect also, the Mediterranean serves as a good training-ground for novices in navigation.

The early mariners used natural navigational aids, they watched the birds fly (a technique echoed in the story of Noah and the dove), or followed the direction of the winds and currents, or checked the nature of the sea bottom. Astronomy, a science closely linked with astrology, was highly developed in prehistoric times, and became the mainstay of Mediterranean navigation at that early date. Prehistoric settlements on the islands and evidence of the exploitation of their resources even before the Neolithic Age point to the existence of seafaring and controlled navigation some 10,000 years ago and even earlier.

With the advance of the Bronze Age, hugging the coast became impractical. As early as the second millennium BC, the Phoenicians were practising direct crossings to the African shores and beyond Gibraltar, although the details of their ventures there were kept secret and have not reached us. They are confirmed by the spread of their colonies west of Gibraltar and by the presence of tin as a major item of their international trade. Through the Red Sea, they carried on regular traffic to Arabia and East Africa. Around 600 BC, they were believed to have circumnavigated Africa, as Herodotus tells us (4:42):

> Africa, except where it borders Asia, is clearly surrounded by water. Necho, Pharaoh of Egypt around 600 BC, was the first we know of to demonstrate this. When he finished digging out the canal between the Nile and the Red Sea [one of the precursors of the Suez Canal], he sent out a naval expedition manned by the Phoenicians, instructing them to come home by way of the straits of Gibraltar into the Med., and in that fashion get back to Egypt. So, setting out from the Red Sea, the Phoenicians sailed into the Indian Ocean. Each autumn they put in at whatever part of Africa they happened to be sailing by, sowed the soil, stayed there until harvest time, reaped the grain, and went on; so that two years passed, and it was not until the third that they rounded the Pillars of Hercules and made it back to Egypt. And they reported things which others can believe if they want, but I cannot, namely that in sailing around Africa they had the sun on the right side.

Other attempts to sail around Africa were made in later generations, usually from west to east, but they all seem to have failed. Around 500 BC, Hanno of Carthage was sent by the Carthaginian authorities down the coast of West Africa, to set up trading colonies there. Running out of provisions (or for other reasons which must remain obscure), he turned back somewhat before the Gulf of Guinea, or at the furthest off Cameroon.

At about the same time, the Greeks were active navigators too, but on a completely different scale. Their legendary feats, described by Homer, are limited by modern research to the straits and capes of the Aegean and Ionian Seas. Odysseus's journey is traced as far west and north as Sardinia, and as far south as Crete. Jason and the Argonauts are believed to have sailed the Black Sea and its eastern shores. There is no agreement about the time and details of these voyages. Unless new data are discovered, the only way we have of verifying these speculations is by actual trial, using ships reconstructed for this purpose. Such voyages have been taken, following the routes of the Odyssey east and west, and of the Argonauts into the Black Sea. These voyages clearly demonstrate the difficulties which ancient craft would have had in beating against the wind and current, especially in the Turkish Straits.

During the Hellenistic period, by 300 BC, Pytheas, a Greek from Marseille, broke through the Carthaginian hold on the western waters and sailed through the Straits of Gibraltar far north to 'Ultima Thule', the end of the world. He visited Britain and Ireland, then went on to Iceland or Norway, a place he described as an icy island. On his way back, he might have explored the coasts of the Baltic or the North Sea. Around 120 BC, another Greek by the name of Eudoxus from Alexandria made two voyages from the Red Sea to India. Twice he came back with a precious cargo of eastern spices, which were confiscated by the authorities on his arrival. The third time he tried to get to the East by sailing around Africa, failed, tried again, and was never heard of thereafter.

In Roman times, the ties with northern Europe and the British Isles were intensified, and eastern routes reached as far as China, although the meeting point was usually India, with occasional crossings to the Malay archipelago. Against this background of a wider world, the Mediterranean became an inner lake, under one rule for the only time in its long history, traversed from end to end by many vessels which plied its waters as a matter of course, carrying merchandise, armies and passengers.

Without compass, chart or chronometer, using such rudimentary methods as the finger or rod to find direction by the sun and stars – principally the Great and Lesser Bears – the ancient Mediterranean mariners were among the first to steer to the horizon, laying the foundations of a continuous seafaring tradition, which is the basis of all modern developments in this field.

The major feature of Mediterranean navigation until the dawn of the modern era was its limitation to only a few months in the year. According to the Roman author Vegetius (4:39), conditions were unstable in March and April, September and October, so seafaring was recommended only during the period from May to mid-September. From December to February, the 'seas are closed'. This pattern is confirmed by medieval sources, which add that it was sometimes enforced by law. Only on special occasions were there sea-crossings in the winter, for urgent dispatches, military operations and food supplies. Ships going overseas in the spring would return in the autumn, and those going in the autumn usually wintered overseas.

The duration of the voyages could be anything from years and months to weeks and days, depending on the winds and the nature of the stop-overs. Even the rowed boats could not exceed 4 knots (a knot is 1 nautical mile, about 2 km, per hour) on the long run, and that indeed was the average speed of a boat under sail in fair wind. Thus the trip from Byblos (in Lebanon) to Egypt could take four days or four months, that from Alexandria to Rome two weeks or half a year, and that beyond Gibraltar from a couple of years to eternity. The hazards from nature and man were enormous both on the high seas and on shore. The high risks involved resulted in exorbitant rates for loans towards maritime enterprises, and for insurance.

The average speed of a vessel today is eight to ten times faster, rather lower than the revolutionary differences on land and in the air; but risk and uncertainty have been cut to a minimum, making maritime traffic one of the least expensive and safest ways of communication.

In antiquity, there was no escape from danger and calamity. Shipwrecks dot the Mediterranean sea-bed by the thousand; although tragedies at the time, they are our best source for the history of seafaring and navigation. From the great variety of goods shipped all over the region, we can deduce the extent of sea-borne trade and the fixed sailing routes, as well as more sporadic contacts. We become familiar with the hardships and continuous dangers which confronted the ancient mariners, though we may only speculate as to the means they employed to overcome them. One accidental discovery of a strange astronomical instrument, however, the so-called 'computer' from Antikythera, points to the technological innovations which must have contributed to the art of navigation. It may be described as a premature astrolabe, designed to help fix the positions of the sun and stars. It had a series of dials which swivelled to indicate the desired positions by means of elaborate gearing. However, it has become known to us through a shipwreck which it failed to prevent.

After the story of the prophet Jonah, the most famous shipwreck in antiquity is that of St Paul, as described in the Acts of the Apostles. It is quoted here at length, because of the wealth of detail concerning the route taken, the ports visited, the prevailing winds, and the procedure taken under stress (Acts 27):

> And when it was determined that we should sail into Italy, they delivered Paul and certain other prisoners unto one named Julius, a centurion of Augustus' band. And entering into a ship of Adramyttium, we launched, meaning to sail by the coasts of Asia. . . . And the next day we touched at Sidon, and Julius courteously entreated Paul, and gave him liberty to go unto his friends to refresh himself. And when we had launched from thence, we sailed under Cyprus, because the winds were contrary. And when we sailed over the sea of Cilicia and Pamphylia, we came to Myra, a city of Lycia. And there the centurion found a ship of Alexandria sailing into Italy, and he put us therein. And when we had sailed slowly for many days, and scarce were come over against Cnidos, the wind not suffering us, we sailed under Crete, over against Salmone.

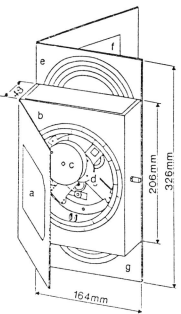

*The astronomical device dubbed 'the computer' of Antikythera, first century BC* (left), *and its reconstruction* (right)

(a) *front door inscription;* (b) *front dial;* (c) *eccentric drum;* (d) *front mechanism;* (e) *four slip rings of upper back dial;* (f) *back door inscription;* (g) *three slip rings of lower back dial.*

*There are more than twenty interlocking gear-wheels set in motion by the input axle (on the right), causing the pointers to move on a set of inscribed dials, which indicate the positions of the sun, the moon and some constellations*

And hardly passing it, came unto a place which is called 'the fair havens'; nigh whereunto was the city of Lasea. Now when much time was spent, and when sailing was now dangerous, because the fast was now already past, Paul admonished them, and said unto them, Sirs, I perceive that this voyage will be with hurt and much damage, not only of the lading and ship, but also of our lives. . . . And because the haven was not commodious to winter in, the more part advised to depart thence also, if by any means they might attain to Phenice, and there to winter. . . . And when the south wind blew softly, supposing that they

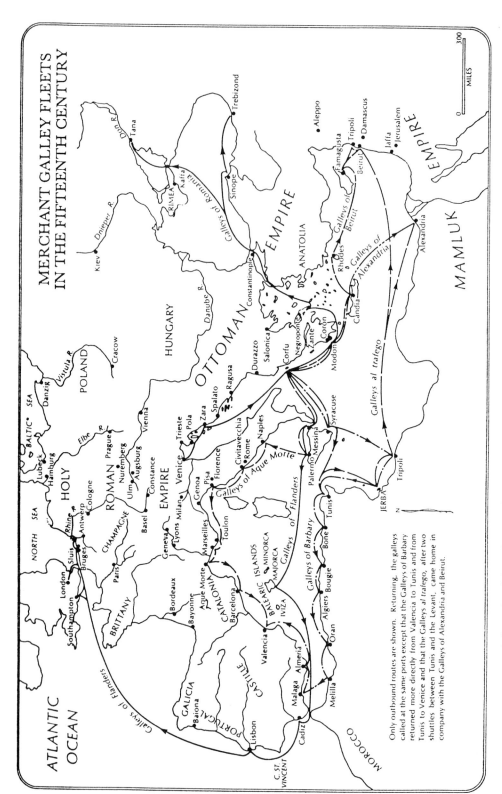

# MERCHANT GALLEY FLEETS
# IN THE FIFTEENTH CENTURY

ATLANTIC
OCEAN

NORTH
SEA

BALTIC SEA

Kiev

Dnieper R.

Don R.

Tana

Trebizond

Kaffa

CRIMEA

Sinope

*Galleys of Romania*

Constantinople

OTTOMAN

EMPIRE

ANATOLIA

Aleppo

Famagusta

Tripoli

Damascus

Beirut

Jaffa

Jerusalem

MAMLUK

EMPIRE

*Galleys of Beirut*

Rhodes

*Galleys of Alexandria*

Candia

Alexandria

Coron

Modon

Zante

Negroponte

Corfu

Salonica

Durazzo

Ragusa

Spalato

Zara

Pola

Trieste

Venice

Milan

Genoa

Pisa

Florence

Lyons

Geneva

Marseilles

Toulon

Civitavecchia

Rome

Naples

Messina

Palermo

Syracuse

*Galleys al tralego*

Tripoli

JERBA

N

*Galleys of Aque Morte*

*Galleys of Flanders*

*Galleys of Barbary*

Tunis

Bone

Bougie

Algiers

Oran

Melilla

Malaga

Almeria

Cadiz

C. ST. VINCENT

Lisbon

Baiona

GALICIA

PORTUGAL

CASTILE

MOROCCO

Valencia

Barcelona

BALEARIC ISLANDS

MINORCA

MAJORCA

IVIZA

CATALONIA

Bayonne

Bordeaux

Ague Morte

BRITTANY

Paris

CHAMPAGNE

Southampton

London

Sluis

Bruges

Antwerp

Cologne

Rhine

Lubeck

Hamburg

Danzig

Vistula R.

POLAND

Cracow

HUNGARY

Vienna

Danube R.

HOLY

ROMAN

EMPIRE

Prague

Nuremberg

Augsburg

Ulm

Constance

Basel

Elbe R.

*Galleys of Flanders*

OTTOMAN EMPIRE

0    300
MILES

Only outbound routes are shown. Returning, the galleys
called at the same ports except that the Galleys of Barbary
returned more directly from Valencia to Tunis and from
Tunis to Venice and that the Galleys al tralego, after two
shuttles between Tunis and the Levant, came home in
company with the Galleys of Alexandria and Beirut.

*Venetian trade lines (mude) at the end of the fifteenth century*

had obtained their purpose, loosing thence, they sailed close by Crete. But not long after there arose against it a tempestuous wind, called Euroclydon. And when the ship was caught, and could not bear up into the wind, we let her drive. And running under a certain island which is called Clauda, we had much work to come by the boat; Which when they had taken up, they used helps, undergirding the ship; and fearing lest they should fall into the quicksands, struck sail, and so were driven. And we being exceedingly tossed with a tempest, the next day they lightened the ship; And the third day we cast out with our own hands the tackling of the ship. And when neither sun nor stars in many days appeared, and no small tempest lay on us, all hope that we should be saved was then taken away. . . . But when the fourteenth night was come, as we were driven up and down in Adria, about midnight the shipmen deemed that they drew near to some country; And sounded, and found it twenty fathoms, and when they had gone a little further, they sounded again, and found it fifteen fathoms. Then fearing lest we should have fallen upon rocks, they cast four anchors out of the stern, and wished for the day. And as the shipmen were about to flee out of the ship, when they had let down the boat into the sea, under colour as though they would have cast anchors out of the foreship, Paul said to the centurion and to the soldiers, Except these abide in the ship, ye cannot be saved. Then the soldiers cut off the ropes of the boat, and let her fall off. And while the day was coming on, Paul besought them all to take meat, saying, This day is the fourteenth day that ye have tarried and continued fasting. . . . And we were in all in the ship two hundred threescore and sixteen souls. And when they had eaten enough, they lightened the ship, and cast out the wheat into the sea. And when it was day, they knew not the land; but they discovered a certain creek with a shore, into the which they were minded, if it were possible, to thrust in the ship. And when they had taken up the anchors, they committed themselves unto the sea, and loosed the rudder bands, and hoisted up the mainsail to the wind, and made toward shore. And falling into a place where two seas met, they ran the ship aground; and the forepart struck fast, and remained unmoveable, but the hinder part was broken with the violence of the waves. And the soldiers' counsel was to kill the prisoners, lest any of them should swim out, and escape. But the centurion, willing to save Paul, kept them from their purpose, and commanded that they which could swim should cast themselves first into the sea, and get to land. And the rest, some on boards, and some on broken pieces of the ship. And so it came to pass, that they escaped all safe to land. And when they were escaped, then they knew that the island was called Melita.

Malta still worships St Paul in a cave in Rabat, not far from the bay bearing his name. In its churches, as in shrines all over the Mediterranean, many votive offerings commemorate traumatic experiences not unlike the one which was described so vividly almost 2,000 years ago. They continue an age-old tradition, found in all Mediterranean cultures, which reached a peak during the eighteenth and nineteenth centuries, mainly in the Catholic West. The votive paintings, which comprise most of the offerings, typically depict the scene of the catastrophe, a ship breaking up on high seas or being blown up during battle. The upper part of the painting contains the image of the saint or saints to whom the vow was made. At the bottom, a short legend gives the date and describes the circumstances. This tradition is far from dying, although it is certainly changing – photographs are now used, and the saints' images tend to disappear. This is an aspect of folk art that is just beginning to be explored, and is a mine of information on popular belief, ethnology and the history of seafaring.

The route taken by St Paul was one of the most widely used throughout the days of sail. To go east, the mariner could depart from any port in the western Mediterranean, and let the north-westerly winds drive him to his destination. To go west was a different story, as he then had to beat against the prevailing winds. Like St Paul's, ships in the eastern Mediterranean used to sail north, then go close to the shore of Asia Minor, and continue westward through the islands. Another major route ran parallel with the North African shore, and there was a further, middle route, among the big islands of the Mediterranean – Cyprus, Crete, Sicily, Sardinia and Majorca. Several important north–south routes had always existed – from southern Anatolia to Egypt, from Greece to Cyrenaica, from Italy to Tunisia, and from Spain to Morocco.

These routes did not change much with time, but their relative importance reflected the political and economic vicissitudes of each era. In classical times, the north–south routes were all-important, maintaining contact between the metropolis and the colonies, feeding capital cities like Athens and Rome. These north–south routes were hardly used in the first centuries after the Muslim conquest, and certainly not for commercial purposes. As the Mediterranean became divided, the Christians in the north used a west-east route close to their coasts, while the Muslims used the one adjacent to theirs.

*A marine compass of the fourteenth century*

The middle route became a no man's land; pirates were most active here. This pattern continued well into the modern era. In the nineteenth century piracy was suppressed, and the opening of the Suez Canal brought much greater importance to the sea lanes in the south-east, which would otherwise have been a stagnant backwater.

A revolutionary period in the nautical sciences began during the Middle Ages and the commercial boom of the twelfth and thirteenth centuries. At the beginning of the fourteenth century, any professional captain would have had at his disposal the three major navigational aids: compass, nautical chart and pilot-book. Each of these had its predecessors in antiquity, but only at this time did they become scientifically co-ordinated and widely available. The compass was the most essential, for it was the basis of the development and use of the other two aids.

Tradition has it that the compass was introduced to the Mediterranean by the Muslims, who learnt its use from the Chinese. A seaman of Amalfi, a port-town in southern Italy which maintained close relations with the Muslims of North Africa in the ninth to the eleventh centuries, is credited with adapting the lodestone for use on board ship. This tradition has not yet been proved to have a solid historical basis. New research has shown that both China and the Mediterranean world used the lodestone for thousands of years in divination and geomancy. Ancient cosmogonies divided the world into eight or sixteen sections – these are depicted on many artifacts – and used the lodestone in their rituals. The sixteen-part divisions are closely related to those of the wind-rose, while astronomical and scientific divisions were usually based on a twelve-part division, related to a circle of 360 degrees. Towards the end of the first millennium AD, China started using the lodestone as an aid to navigation, while the oldest western description dates from 1190:

> Sailors . . . when in cloudy weather they can no longer profit by the light of the sun, or when the world is wrapped up in the darkness of the shades of night . . . touch the magnet with a needle. This then whirls around in a circle until, when its motion ceases, its point looks directly to the north.

The true mariner's compass – a direction chart pivoted on a needle and set on gimbals which neutralize the movement of the ship – became standard during the thirteenth century. Encasing the contraption in a box was a crucial addition, which made it durable and portable. In many languages, including Arabic, the term for compass is derived from *bussola*, the Italian for box. Another important addition was the lubber line, indicating on the box the longitudinal axis of the ship; by this the steersman could make his course good.

In fair weather, mariners continued to rely on celestial observations, so at first the compass served mainly in emergencies and in bad weather; it contributed to the increase in the turnover of goods, as the ships did not have to wait for ideal weather conditions. It was essential to the development of another major navigational aid of the time – the nautical chart or *portolano*, which also appeared around the turn of the fourteenth century; the earliest version we know is the Carta Pisana of *c.* 1275. These maps, works of art as much as scientific instruments, constitute a turning point in the history of cartography. For the first time, they combined scale with orientation,

*A medieval Muslim marine astrolabe* (left)*, and the western European directions for its use* (right)

emphasizing the wind-rose as the heart of the map. They were oddly shaped; the coast was dotted with innumerable harbours and anchorages, while inland there was hardly any detail, except for decorative drawings of major urban centres. These new trends in cartography had a direct impact on the development of other sciences, and made their contribution to the spirit of the Renaissance.

Together with the compass and the nautical chart, mariners used a written guide, very similar to the modern pilot-book. The Greeks called this kind of book a *periplos* (sailing around), and one survives from the first century AD, describing the western Indian Ocean or Erythraean Sea. The tradition was all but lost in the West until the spread of literacy and the expansion of seafaring, based on accurate measurements, revived it. A description of the port of Acre, found in the earliest of these compilations, may serve the modern pilot as well. *Lo compasso de navegare* was written in Italian, and completed by the middle of the thirteenth century:

> From the White Cape to the city of Acre it is ten miles to the south-west; when you reach the shoals opposite Casal Imbert [modern Akhziv], turn a bit to the south-east; from this shoal to Acre there are several reefs, at two and three miles. Acre is a bay and a good port. There is a reef there which makes the port. You may stay anchored by this reef at a depth of four paces [about 7 m]. Towards the land there is the 'Tower of Flies', and the entrance to the said port is between the tower and the reef. When you approach the port, keep at a distance of 3 log-line knots [about 50 m] from the headquarters of the Templars and the church of St Andrew, because of the reef which stretches beyond the church. When you observe the house which used to belong to the Constable on the right of the Tower of Flies, you may sail straight into the port. When you enter the port, steer in with the city of Haifa on the east of the stern and the Tower of Flies on mid prow, this way you sail into the port avoiding that shoal.

At the same time, other developments were gathering momentum. Mediterranean contacts with the Atlantic and Indian Oceans had been severed with the disintegration of the Roman Empire and the knowledge of their seafaring traditions was lost. Only in the High Middle Ages, due to the crusading and missionary movements and to the intensive commercial activity of the times, did mariners resume sailing and exploring east and north. Greek and Muslim traditions were revived at the universities which were founded everywhere at the time. The maritime heritage was especially nurtured by scholarly circles in Spain and Portugal, where during the fourteenth and fifteenth centuries scientists found a synthesis between the practical knowledge of the mariners and the latest achievements of Muslim, Jewish and Christian research in this field.

As well as excellent charts, these scholars produced the first of a long line of measuring instruments, Jacob's staff (or cross-staff), whose invention is attributed to the Spanish Jew Levi Ben Gershon. This instrument, like the quadrant and others which followed it, provided a simple way of reading the altitude of the stars by measuring the angle formed between the line running from them to the beholder and the horizon line, from which the exact latitude could be calculated. This invention may also have come from China to the West, carried by Muslim travellers: the Kemal (similar to the cross-staff) could have been the link in this chain. Another instrument which was certainly developed by the Muslims and passed on to Christian mariners was the astrolabe, an ancient astronomical device converted to marine usage by the end of the Middle Ages. Extant specimens are a combination of beauty and efficiency. Correcting the course when navigating under adverse circumstances was done with the help of another device, the Tavola de Martelojo (a form of traverse table): given the direction in which the ship was forced to sail by contrary winds or currents, the distance covered and the desired destination, a mariner could calculate with this table the correction needed to make his course good.

Establishing position was not imperative for the Mediterranean mariner. He knew his direction, and if necessary, found his rough position by deduced calculation, distorted to dead reckoning, and based on approximate speed and sailing time. In the wider oceans it was a major problem. After finding the latitude, longitude remained unsolved. As this could not easily be defined by astronomical observations, it depended on accurate time being kept on board – a difficult task when an hour-glass, which usually lasted only half an hour, had to be constantly watched and turned, and was never precise. Only in the eighteenth century, with the perfection of the chronometer, was this problem satisfactorily solved. Many new aids for seafarers have been devised; the most important contribution to navigation in modern times has been radar, but even today, with satellite navigation and computerized weather routing, mariners will not go to sea without their favourite manual instrument, usually the sextant.

Going beyond the horizon meant much more than reaching new lands, opening new markets, spreading the gospel. With an open horizon, there was always room for the search for Eden, the Kingdom of Prester John, the Lost Tribes, Eldorado. The world was endless, shapeless, full of mystery, fear and hope. Only the closing of the frontiers, the rounding up of all the horizons, gave man a true concept of the world around him and of his proper place in it. This could not be achieved without the crossing of the oceans, which, of course happened outside the Mediterranean. Many navigational aids which had their origin in the Far East were perfected in the Atlantic by northern mariners, but it was the Mediterranean which served as the laboratory, where navigation was rehearsed and its rules and tools adapted and developed. Today, navigation can hardly be improved any further. On the surface, the ocean planet is known and conquered by man. Now we are witnessing the beginning of a new nautical revolution – where we add a third dimension by penetrating the oceans' depths and navigating on the sea bottom.

## CHAPTER 8

# LIFE ON BOARD

'THERE ARE THREE KINDS of people in the world: the living, the dead, and those who go to sea.' This dictum, ascribed to Anacharsis the Scythian of the sixth century BC, well reflects the landlubber's attitude to life on board ship, and the conditions of life at sea until very recent times. Modern technology has so changed life at sea that it is hard even to imagine the conditions on board ship in the days before steam and steel, electricity and refrigeration. The modern craft is a cross between a good hotel and an industrial plant, to the point where even the weather, the decisive factor in mariners' lives in the past, concerns the shipping company and its scheduling system more than it does the individual seaman. The modern farmer, equipped with all kinds of machinery, still gets up every morning of his life looking at the sky and checking the weather, while the modern seaman seems to be less sensitive to it than an outdoor cameraman.

Until the dawn of the modern era, maritime activity in the Mediterranean was limited to five months out of the year, and seafarers were laid off for the remaining months, either at home or beyond the sea, wherever they happened to land and spend the winter. During the sailing season, there were many long stopovers in various ports, either to deal with the cargo or because of weather conditions. Today, the need for intensive turnover and the high cost of delays have cut port-time to a minimum. In many cases, seamen hardly go ashore. From this point of view, in spite of the differences, service on a modern cargo ship is still, as in times past, only for those who can endure being cooped up for weeks and months, away from land and home.

In the past, people became seamen out of economic necessity, but the urge to get away and see the world played an important role. With modern communications and tight schedules, there is little room for fantasy. Instability in the shipping world often causes protracted lay-offs, which mariners today do not accept as they did in antiquity. This is one of the reasons why crews all over the world now have a heavy component of Third

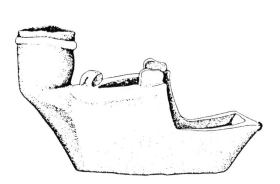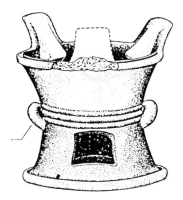

*Roman ship stoves from the second to first century BC:* (left) *lead;* (right) *terracotta*

World nationals, mostly from the Far East. These foreign hands are usually hired *ad hoc* and do not belong to any labour union. Seamen on the payrolls of their national lines rarely spend their entire life at sea. In most cases, they stay on board for a few years, then quit or go into early retirement, and the premature loss of experienced seamen weakens the whole system.

Literary sources do not tell us much about sailors in ancient times and their life on board. They were usually illiterate, and nobody else was interested enough in them to leave a written description. Here again, the finds of underwater archaeology shed light on a hitherto little known aspect of seafaring. In many of the excavated shipwrecks, the galley at the stern has been well preserved, with many of the personal belongings of the crew. From the amount and nature of the kitchenware found, we may deduce the size of the crew and their social standing. Clay vessels were also used for lighting and heating. Special items – a measuring rod, a wine thief used to syphon wine out of a sealed amphora, a tool set, armoury pieces – tell us something about the crew's occupations and manners. The remains of their food are testimony to their diet and sometimes even to their religious affiliation. The biggest concern on board was fire, which probably took the heaviest toll of the old wooden boats. On the seventh-century ship found at Yassi-Ada, the kitchen was equipped with a tiled stove, and was situated partly above deck for ventilation. Many portable stoves and heaters were found elsewhere, in the form of stocking-shaped containers, made of clay or lead, sometimes with double sides, for water. Besides the crew, most ancient ships had craftsmen

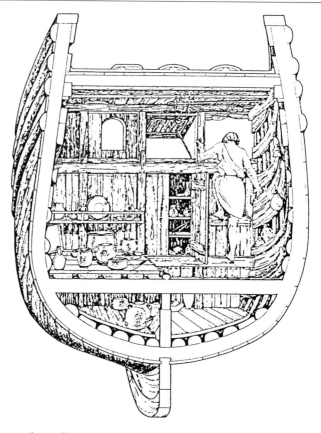

*A Byzantine ship galley reconstructed from the finds in the seventh-century AD shipwreck of Yassi-Ada, Turkey*

on board: a smith, a glass blower, a physician, certainly a shipwright and later on a caulker. These craftsmen usually carried their tools with them. In the Phoenician ship newly found off the Israeli coast a complete shipwright's tool-kit was discovered, although the ship seems to have been brand-new.

There were no specific sleeping quarters. As sailing was a fair weather occupation, seamen usually slept on deck, or under cover of an old sail. In severe conditions, they would crawl in with the merchandise below deck, if there was one. There was sometimes a cabin aft, for the captain and on occasion also for his mates. Officers' quarters were moved to the fore only after the introduction of steam. Before that time, the expression 'to serve before the mast' meant doing the simple jobs of an ordinary seaman. The average freighter in antiquity, of 30 to 50 tonnes, would have four to ten seamen aboard. The regular ratio was about one man to 5 tonnes capacity, while the more sophisticated systems of sails in the early modern period could do with one man to 10 tonnes of cargo. Big cargo vessels of hundreds of tonnes had dozens of men aboard, and living conditions were very crowded. For thousands of years, sailors have been handling sails; now they are simply seamen, servicing the engines and the ship in general. As automation sets in, crews have become very small, with a ratio of about one man to 5,000 tonnes capacity. While the crew grows smaller, the ship grows bigger, resembling an empty ghost compared to the crowded bedlam of yore.

From papyri sources of the second millennium BC we get the first glimpse of the sailors' diet. Bread rations were listed as the staple food on board. With time, seamen learnt to prepare a special twice-baked bread (*biscoctum*, ship's biscuit) made from an extra-durable kind of wheat. In addition to bread, they had olives, dates and raisins, the pits of which were found on almost every wreck dating from 500 BC to AD 500. Sometimes they cooked fish or meat, which had usually been preserved by salting, with pulses such as beans and lentils. Hard cheese was added to the diet on occasion. Fresh water was kept in big clay containers and was used also to dilute the wine.

This basic diet did not change for thousands of years, as is indicated by written evidence from the beginning of the fourteenth century AD. The Venetian Marino Sanudo the elder, writing a detailed proposal for a new crusade in 1321, calculated the expenses involved, including feeding the navy. Frederick Chapin Lane, the specialist in Venetian maritime history, came to the conclusion that crews in the Middle Ages were reasonably well fed. They received some 4,000 calories and over 100 grams of protein a day, made up of bread, wine, beans, cheese and salt pork. Scurvy was not a problem because of the frequent stops along the way, where fresh fruit and vegetables were plentiful.

Generally, ancient mariners did not work for wages. They were partners in a joint venture, for better or for worse. The ship was divided into shares or spaces, and each mariner had one or more of them. They all had their say in matters such as decisions on the course to be taken, changes of itinerary, additional investments and charters. The profits were shared according to traditional rules, whereby the owner of the ship received one half, and the other half went to the crew, with the captain getting two parts, the helmsman one and a half, and each of the mariners one part of the net profit.

This typical Mediterranean co-operative spirit arose from the specific circumstances of sea voyages and took account of the hostility of both nature and man, as well as crude navigation. The disadvantage of this system was a lack of discipline, which under stress could be quite dangerous.

Co-operation is clearly reflected in the ancient maritime codes, especially the Rhodian sea-law, of which it is the underlying principle (see Chapter 9). At the same time, the owner of the ship or a representative of the owner was usually the captain as well, and managed the financial and commercial aspects of the trading venture. In Greek he was called *naucleros*, and we can trace him in the Yassi-Ada seventh-century wreck, where the measuring rods are marked 'Georgios Presbiteros' – the elder. This tradition continued in the medieval world, both Muslim and Christian. In the documents of the Geniza and the Italian cities' archives, many shipowners, who tramped with their vessels all around the Mediterranean, buying and selling together with their crews, are mentioned by name, and it is possible for us to follow their careers, at least in part.

In Roman Imperial times, the system was different. Accumulated wealth and the growing volume of maritime trade made for a separation of functions and a more formal and authoritative set up. The ship became an investment, and its owner seldom travelled on board. Instead, his representative would charter the ship to several merchants, and hire a captain to sail the ship under his command. The crew consisted of hired hands or slaves. With the disintegration of the Western Empire in the fourth century and the rise of Byzantium in the East, shipping reverted to its pre-Roman structure. It was the commercial and nautical revolution of the late Middle Ages which changed this pattern drastically.

From the thirteenth century on, in addition to the *patrono* (the owner's representative, or shipmaster), the *nocchiero* (sailing master), and the *marinari*, there would also be a *scriba*, the ship's clerk, who made sure everything was carried out in accordance with the law and custom of the sea. He kept the ship's register, which included various contracts, bills of lading, customs clearance, the log-book, the lists of crew and passengers, and was responsible to the authorities. The crew were hired on the quays by a handshake and registered by the scribe, for the trip or for the season; they received wages instead of a share of the profits. The mariners usually got an advance payment, to last their families until their return. Many ran away with the money, so that a good part of the ancient maritime codes dealt with their salaries and obligations.

In those days, mariners were allowed to trade individually on the side, and the profit they made was sometimes double their wages. Tax reductions or exemptions for seamen, probably descending from this practice, are the expression of the authorities' intention to subsidize the profession, although smuggling and illegal trade have always been the rule rather than the exception. The development of the microelectronic industry brought a new boom in this field; some lines have been dubbed by the authorities the 'Seiko Line' or the 'Sanyo Line', after the quantities of watches and transistor radios smuggled through them. But the petty illegal trade of seamen is negligible in comparison with today's huge maritime frauds, such as emptying a tanker or dropping a container, that may involve millions of pounds.

While the status of the mariners as partners in the sea venture deteriorated to that of wage-earners, the nautical revolution widened the gap between captain and crew by making a sound theoretical knowledge of cartography and other nautical sciences essential for higher posts; this was far more demanding than the previous practical experience required. Very often, the captain was the only person on board who actually owned the new instruments. As voyages became longer and more adventurous, there could be no recourse to authorities on land for long periods of time. The old Mediterranean spirit of the sea voyage as a joint venture gave way to another concept, with the captain as the omnipotent ruler of his little kingdom – the ship – for better or worse. Interestingly, the captain has retained his authoritative position until the present, although the direct responsibility for navigating a sea-going vessel has long since passed to his first mate, and has recently been taken over by the computer on board.

Mediterranean pirates were the last keepers of the old tradition. Their laws and customs, which dealt with issues such as the distribution of profits, rules of conduct on board ship and during battle, even remuneration for invalidity caused by piratical action, reflect the general air of equality and informality prevalent in the old days.

Handling a ship today is a sophisticated procedure, highly mechanized and electronically controlled, so the seamen have to be properly trained professionals. Gone are the days of the 'Shanghai' practice, whereby drunken sailors were collected from the bars to find themselves in the midst of the ocean, on a voyage lasting several months. Among the costs of maritime transportation, that of the labour force is becoming decisive, and much effort is spent today to limit this expense and render the crew more effective. Increasing automation has made it possible for a ship of about 50,000 tonnes to be handled by ten to twenty men. The clear-cut division between engine and deck is disappearing, and most seamen serve as 'GPs' – General Purpose.

These developments have a bearing on the captain's authority. He can no longer use the terrible punishments known from the earlier days of ocean crossings, which in any case never seemed to suit the Mediterranean character. While the captain's authority is more limited, his responsibility is much heavier, for the vessel and cargo entrusted to him are usually worth many millions of pounds, and he is also answerable to charges of an ecological and political nature (spills and stowaways, for instance). As crews are so restricted in number and so highly qualified, relationships on board tend to be much less formal, with team-work and solidarity replacing distrust and distance. The tendency is to have the ships run by a managerial unit, which aims to develop a highly motivated group spirit. Even the age-old separation of officers from crew is mellowing into more of a family atmosphere, supported by common sports and pastimes. Video tape reports keep the seamen informed of news within the company and enhance their further personal involvement with it, as well as bringing them messages from family and friends. Thus the original Mediterranean spirit of solidarity on board is being revived in the latest methods of crew management.

The basic problems facing seamen today are the same as those which have existed since antiquity. The organizations in charge of seamen's welfare take care both of the seaman on board and of his family on shore. No matter how well decorated and equipped, the ship is still a confined space, with tensions and drudgery an inseparable part of it. In the past, sailors used to engage in all kinds of crafts – wood and ivory carving, model making and the like. Today these occupations are no longer followed, due in part to the tighter schedule, while television has somewhat curtailed social contact, though this survives. One problem is that, like other closed environments, the ship is corrupting inasmuch as it takes care of all one's needs. Seamen are frequently reluctant to leave their asylum and are badly conditioned for life on land.

The family of the seaman has a special structure. It is the eternal triangle – the man, his wife and the sea. The men serve their term on board for three to four months, then stay at home for about the same length of time. When they have to go out again, it is always the wrong time – a new baby is born or a holiday approaching. Under stress, the wife tends to blame the company, rather than her husband, for her desertion. In her daily life alone, she is almost independent, heading a single-parent family. Many seamen's wives tend to keep problems and bad news to themselves, rather than burden the husband, who cannot help anyway; he then blames himself and suffers from a chronic guilt complex. Now seamen's families are encouraged to involve the men as much as possible in their daily life, whatever the cost, because in the long run this works much better both on shore and on board.

Around the ports, there is another class of people who are an essential component of seafaring life, namely the stevedores, crane-operators, divers (for salvage) and clerks. In antiquity, most of these were slaves, who could not go on strike. As freemen in the Middle Ages, they were organized in guilds, but economic ups and downs were considered to be an act of God rather than the results of evil-doing on the part of the rich or the government. Today their counterparts are so well organized that they can paralyse a nation's international commerce.

In the past, the crews of the merchant marine and the navy were the same people, for separate and permanent navies did not exist until the modern period. On merchantmen as well as on warships, each seaman was supposed to bring his personal arms with him. They usually consisted of sword, dagger, lance, shield, helmet and breastplate. Mates had additional weapons and superior body armour. Before the use of firearms was developed, the crew was the vessel's principal armament, and the distinction between armed and unarmed vessels lay in the number of men aboard. Even oared ships in the Mediterranean relied mainly on their sails, and the large crews did not serve to increase speed. They were aboard in order to enter a port or leave, to get ahead in a calm and of course during battle.

In order to man the oars on fighting ships, in ancient Greece as in medieval Italy, oarsmen were recruited by lot or quota from the general seagoing population. This service implied a social standing and expressed much patriotic pride, but sometimes was commuted to a money payment. Greek naval warfare depended on manoeuvres (such as ramming), demanding a high degree of training, solidarity and motivation, which were fully appreciated (*The Old Oligarch*, 1:2):

> In the first place, I maintain, it is only just that the poorer classes and the common people of Athens should be better off than the men of birth and wealth, seeing that it is the people who man the fleet and have brought the city her power. The steersman, the boatswain, the lieutenant, the lookout man in the prow, the shipwright – these are the people who supply the city with power far rather than her heavy infantry and men of birth and quality.

These qualities were certainly hard to find among slaves. It is true that under Rome the fleets were manned mostly by slaves, for the fighting was done by the marines on board. Even captains were frequently slaves in Roman times. But during the long period of warfare between Islam and Christianity, all through the Middle Ages, the men at the oars of the war fleets were free citizens. It was in this period that naval organization and hierarchy were consolidated. The terminology of the seafarer – words like admiral and

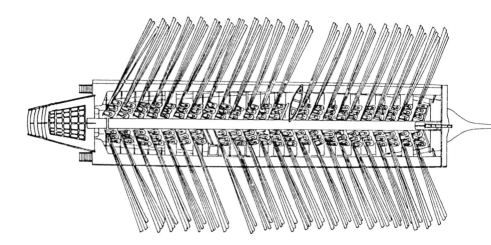

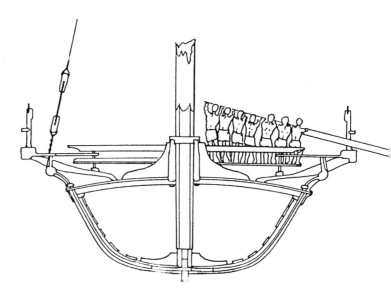

*Oarsmen on a galley at the end of the Middle Ages:* (top) *with individual oars arranged in groups of three (a terzaruolo);* (below and right) *with, heavy oars rowed by groups of men (a scaloccio)*

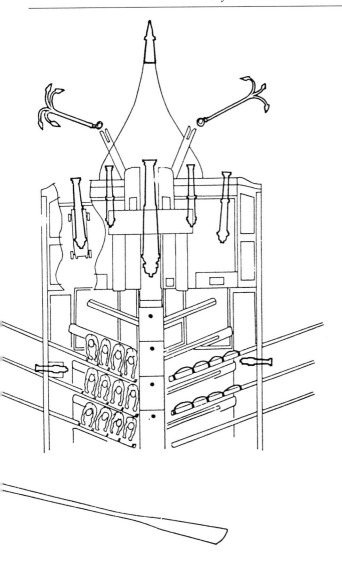

captain, armada and flotilla – stems from Greek and Latin, Arabic and Italian sources, and reflects Mediterranean conditions at the time.

Medicine on board was a pioneering field, which developed in the Italian navy and merchant fleet. In 1318 a renowned physician and surgeon founded in Venice the first home for aged or ailing seamen.

On stepping ashore, oarsmen returned to their other marine-related occupations. The wages of the lowest paid oarsman were the equivalent of the earnings of an unskilled labourer on land, but his income was increased by trading and by war booty. Oarsmen were entitled to use their benches, on which they sat and slept, for storing wares to trade as well.

But at the end of the Middle Ages, when archers and crossbowmen started challenging the supremacy of the mounted knight, oarsmen began to lose their status. The bows, as well as the armament needed against the deadly arrows, were too expensive for the common seaman, and the use of the bows required specialized training. As they gradually lost their usefulness as fighters and their trading opportunities, they came to be considered inferior. When seamen reached dire poverty, they would take their advance pay and then jump ship. Arrested, they would claim they had nothing with which to pay their debt, and would be returned to the shipmasters to work for it. While oarsmen were turned into *forcats* (forced labourers), seamen turned into something like a marine proletariat, and tried to better their condition by outbursts of revolt, but to no avail.

The epidemic of the Black Death in the 1350s reduced manpower even further, while the added weight of cannon, which had started to appear on board at the same period, necessitated more manpower, which was now becoming scarce. In the first half of the fourteenth century, at the peak of medieval Mediterranean commercial and naval activity, tens of thousands of *galeoti* (gallery oarsmen) had been needed each season. Conscripted convicts and prisoners of war rowed in units, where only one man was a professional, and the rest followed his stroke. At the battle of Lepanto, the rowers on the Christian side were captive Turks, and on the Turkish side, Christian prisoners.

Ironically, popular images regarding galley slaves date from the seventeenth century, when the time of the galleys was in fact almost at an end. In these late galleys, only the fore and aft areas were decked over, and served as storage space, sick room and officers' quarters. The latter were becoming more elaborate, while the oarsmen's conditions of life and work were deplorable. They were chained to each other, as well as to their benches, which were arranged among the cannon. In an area of less than 5 m by 3 m,

*Disembarking pilgrims in the Holy Land, fifteenth century AD*

five oarsmen lived and worked. One slept on the bench and the others on deck. While they were working, their mouths were stopped with corks which hung around their necks. Although they rowed in shifts, the death rate was very high. Along the middle of the boat ran the bridge, for the officers; the stench was so terrible, that they would cover their faces as they passed. On shore, the *galeoti* were kept in the local prison.

Slaves for sale were mainly transported by galleys, and their conditions seem to have been better than those of the galley slaves. The rule was one slave per tonne, so the gangs did not usually exceed two hundred or so for each boat. Public opinion, which was instrumental in the abolition of slavery at the beginning of the nineteenth century, also did away with galley slaves.

Besides the crew, passengers were an inseparable part of life on board ship, much more so than nowadays. It is usually these travellers who have left us their accounts of ship and crew, itinerary and ports. The most common passengers on board were the merchants. For a certain amount of cargo loaded, they were entitled to free transportation with their personal belongings, servants and provisions. They were sometimes required, like members of the crew, to be properly armed. Some of them were of humble status, but with a long and varied experience at sea, while others were of high social status; these spent time at sea as an essential part of their business and political or military career. In the medieval maritime city states, the ruling class was usually composed of men who combined these three occupations.

Benedetto Zaccaria, a Genoese admiral and merchant (c. 1240–1307), is an outstanding example of such a man. A merchant from a noble family, he became famous as he defended Genoese economic interests on the island of Chios in the turbulent Aegean, whereupon Michael Paleologos (the first Byzantine emperor of this dynasty, which ruled Constantinople until its fall to the Turks) made him his representative in Italy. Just before the fall of the crusader kingdom in the Holy Land, he established a Genoese colony in Tripoli, Lebanon. Following Genoa's close relations with Spain, he served the kings of Castile and Aragon at a period when they were engaged in intensive maritime activity. At the end of his career, he helped found the French navy, just before the outbreak of the Hundred Years War between France and England. All this while he carried on an international trade in alum (a mineral essential to the dyeing process, quarried by the Genoese in Focea, opposite Chios), slaves and other lucrative goods. His activity was wholly international, in the terms of his time.

Government officials and religious dignitaries were another category of passengers. They were usually transported by special oared carriers, which were several times more expensive than the sailing ships, but much safer and more comfortable as they put to port quite frequently. In Roman times, the wealthy used to go on pleasure trips, the luxury of which is beyond belief even in comparison with modern pleasure cruises. There were gilded rooms and shaded promenades, sumptuous women's quarters, dining salons, baths with mosaic floors and pools with bronze statues, floating shrines, vines and fruit trees and continuous entertainment. In the ancient world, simple folk travelled to oracles and shrines, for their health or to attend great festivals. The monotheistic religions converted this habit of travel into pilgrimages to the Holy Places – Jews would go to Jerusalem, Christians to Compostela,

Rome or the Holy Land, Muslims would perform the Hagg to Mecca. Many of them travelled by sea, at least part of their way.

Until the nineteenth century, there were no special passenger lines. People went to the waterfront and looked for a ship going in their direction. Most of them used the freighters, where they were given some space between decks. They would put their mattresses on their luggage, and would be fed by the captain. What with the rats, the stink of the bilge water, and the general filth of the crowd, any trip would be quite an ordeal. The merchants tried to limit the number of pilgrims on board, so usually they totalled around fifty, but at times the number of passengers would reach several hundred.

During periods of great immigration and movements, such as the crusades, there were special vehicles for human transportation which carried over a thousand people in a two or three decker of some 30 m by 7 m and 200 tonnes capacity. The worst refugee ships in modern times may be compared to those ships, often laden with young and old, men and women, as well as with a considerable amount of livestock and other provisions. Most of the passengers were landsmen, who feared the sea. This business reached the proportions of a racket at the end of the Middle Ages, when shipmasters competed in various ways to cheat and abuse poor pilgrims, in spite of repeated legislation.

Sailors and oarsmen, merchants and travellers, were the mainstay of the Mediterranean sea-centred world. The most striking expression of this unity was the language used on and around the sea. In the fifteenth century, the *lingua franca* of the Levant was made up of Greek, Italian, Arabic and Turkish components, with traces of other influences. On smaller craft and in local ports, it is still in use today. Undoubtedly, other such concoctions existed at different periods in Mediterranean history, as in the elAmarna Age and the Hellenistic period. Another language is being formed today, with English asserting its position in the international communication systems.

Now there are fewer seamen than in times past, for in spite of the expansion of maritime transportation, less manpower is needed, although it has to be of a superior quality. Oarsmen have fortunately disappeared, except in rowing competitions, which preserve some of the dynamic solidarity of old times without their gruesome aspects. Passengers have all but disappeared from the sea-lanes, while Roman-style pleasure cruises are gaining ground. It is ironic that the Mediterranean cruises, part of whose appeal is their resemblance to a pilgrimage, are very remote from one in reality. The ships sail by night, and every day is crowded with another historical site to see. Yet even this rushed pace is preferable to the charter aeroplane tours, for the right way to approach things Mediterranean is by sea: landing from heaven is reserved for saints and fallen gods.

At least 50 per cent of the cruiser crowd are women. In the past, they were an exception on board, and were usually kept in closed quarters. Professional seamanship generally is one of the last occupations which still excludes women. Nevertheless, women are edging their way into sailing, surfing, diving, and other marine-related occupations. Honor Frost, an English-woman, is one of the most active pioneering underwater archaeologists in Mediterranean waters. Another woman diver, Guilia d'Angelo, known as *La donna del mare* is a journalist, and directs the most important international marine bookshop, Il Mare of Rome. Colette Zeruya was the head of the Israel Oceanographic Institute, and many other women are conducting research in maritime institutions all over the Mediterranean. However, the liberation of the average Mediterranean woman, both Christian and Muslim, is still a long way off, contrary to the impression one may get from the fashions on the beach.

At the end of the twentieth century in the Mediterranean the popularity of yachting is outstanding. A century ago this was the privilege of the very rich; now yachting is widely prevalent. Yachts can be chartered; in some cases, several people or families share a yacht, while sometimes the yacht has become almost a substitute for the family. Life centres around the boat, not as a means of subsistence, but as a kind of cult. Marinas have become a world apart, with their own population, way of life, economics and mythology. There are now over 100,000 boats moored in Mediterranean marinas in the summer, and over 50 per cent of these belong to inlanders – Germans and Austrians. Although only about 10 per cent of them remain for the winter, thousands of extra mooring spaces are added every year to old and new marinas.

Another manifestation of the urge to fight the sea with minimal means and to harness its forces for sheer pleasure is the fast-spreading epidemic of windsurfing. Far from fearing the sea, people crave its presence. The traditional Mediterranean beach holiday, passively taking in the sun and salty water, has turned into an active experience of life afloat in these ancient waters.

CHAPTER 9

# THE LAW OF THE SEA

T HE SEA, by its nature, is common to all – *'mare natura omnibus patet'*. This dictum of Roman law lies at the basis of maritime law today. The sea had no boundaries, so it became the source of the concept of international law. However, maritime law and custom is a very wide field, which may be roughly divided into three main sectors. The private sector deals with loans and contracts, the legal rights and obligations of the crew, the legal status and accountability of the ship and cargo, cases of shipwreck and other damages. Local marine legislation covers port procedures, taxes and dues, foreign merchants, staple goods, and trade organization in general. International maritime law is concerned with territorial waters, fishing and the exploitation rights of other marine resources, and conduct in war and peace. The history of the origins and development of maritime law in the Mediterranean may be traced back some 5,000 years, and the issues at stake during each period reflect the political, military and economic conditions prevalent at the time.

In the twentieth century, new resources and uses of the seawater, the continental shelf and the sea bottom have been discovered and developed (see Chapter 3); old colonial empires have crumbled and new national states are claiming their rights; two world wars have posed fresh challenges, while global economic interdependence has advanced enormously. The necessary review of the international law of the sea was laid down in the Hague codification conference of 1930, and the work continued in the United Nations conferences held since 1958. In December 1982, the UN Convention on the New Law of the Sea was declared, after a long conference which had lasted since 1973. This latest convention gives an exhaustive coverage of all the major issues at stake today, and lays the foundations for a rational future interrelation between man and the sea.

A preoccupation with the definition of territorial waters goes back some 4,000 years, to one of the first maritime disputes which has come down to us.

Some time around 1130 BC, an Egyptian priest named Wenamon compiled a report about a business trip he had taken; he had been sent by the priests of the temple of Amon in Upper Egypt to purchase a load of cedar wood in Lebanon, for the building of a ceremonial barge. He went down the Nile delta and departed in the spring, to go north on the great sea. His first port of call was Dor, just south of the Carmel Range, where a tribe of sea people called Tjekker had established themselves. Their ruler received the Egyptian envoy with bread, wine and meat. Everything seemed to go well, until one of Wenamon's own men made off with all the gold and silver he had taken for buying the timber in Lebanon and to cover the trip's expenses. Wenamon hurried to the prince of Dor and exclaimed 'I have been robbed in your harbour, and since you are prince of this place, you should start an investigation to look for my money.' The prince replied 'I do not care how important a person you are. I refuse to recognize your complaint. . . . If it had been a thief who belonged to my land. . . . I would have paid it to you from my treasury. . . . But the thief belongs to you! He belongs to your ship! Spend a few days here visiting me, so that I may look for him.' A week passed, Wenamon got impatient and left Dor. Somewhere between Tyre and Byblos he solved his problem by a desperate move. He robbed some Tjekker of their silver, saying 'I am taking your silver, and it will stay with me until you find my silver or the thief who stole it. Even though you did not steal mine, I am taking yours.' His troubles continued in Byblos, where the local prince did not want to get into trouble with the Tjekker, who must have complained to him about Wenamon's robbery. He did not allow Wenamon to get into the harbour for almost a month, then made him send back to Egypt for an additional cargo of goods to pay for the difference in the price of the timber. All this took about eight months, and when the day finally arrived, and the ship laden with timber was about to leave port, eleven Tjekker warships arrived on the scene. Wenamon could do nothing but sit on the beach and cry, but the shrewd prince of Byblos said to the Tjekker 'I cannot arrest a messenger of Amon in my territory, so let me send him off and then you can go after him to arrest him.' Wenamon was saved this time by a south-easterly gale, which drove him to the coast of Alashiya (probably Cyprus), but at this point the papyrus breaks off, cutting short the end of the story.

Wenamon, who received this treatment, was a high ranking official. Rank and file merchants and travellers must have found themselves in situations much worse than his. In a world which recognized only territorial and community law, the stranger had no protection whatsoever. It is not surprising, therefore, that rules pertaining to the status of foreigners were the first international agreements of a civil nature known in history. They usually followed the cessation of a war. They also applied to people arriving by land, but their main importance was in regard to maritime commerce with faraway lands.

In the Assyrian and Hittite Empires of the second millennium BC, foreign merchants usually constituted a *carum*, a foreign colony; these have recently been dubbed a 'trading diaspora'. The local authorities pledged by treaty to protect these foreigners, to give them freedom of movement and of cult, and sometimes to relax the customs and dues for them. In the Greek world, a special official looked after their affairs, the *proxenos*. In Athens, he was a foreign citizen permanently residing in the city, who was officially acknowledged as the representative of his countrymen.

This post was the nucleus of the modern office of consul, which still deals mainly with commercial and cultural relations and has no real connection to its namesake in ancient Rome. In Rome, the equivalent of the Greek *proxenos* was the *praetor peregrinus*, a high official in charge of disputes involving foreigners. The direct origins of the modern consulate may be found in the medieval trading colonies of the Italian maritime towns. Pisa, Genoa and Venice, as well as many others, appointed a consul (sometimes called by a different title) to represent them overseas and head the community of their citizens resident abroad. In addition, he also served as the channel through which the local rulers dealt with the foreign citizens of the particular community. In the Muslim world, a similar post was usually held by a local government appointment, the *wakīl at-tuggar*, a prominent public figure. From the Mediterranean, this system first spread inland, and then, at the beginning of the modern era, all over the world.

Ancient Greece initiated another important commercial institution. In Athens there were maritime courts, the *nautodikai*, which dealt exclusively with litigation involving foreign merchants. These courts had a special quick procedure – they were obliged to give a verdict within a month – and special deterrent powers – they could impose sentences of imprisonment and heavy financial guarantees. In the Middle Ages, a similar institution existed in the crusader kingdoms called 'the Court of the Chain', after the chain which closed the harbour entrance in most medieval ports. They obviously dealt with cases of maritime commercial disputes, and had their own judges and procedure. The English Admiralty court which, since its foundation in the seventeenth century, became the mainstay of international maritime law, had very much the same characteristics.

The so-called Rhodian Sea Law, the oldest maritime code to survive, is also of Greek origin. Incorporated into the Byzantine Basilica some time in the tenth century, it was a repository of customary law for a community lacking national boundaries – the international community of mariners and maritime traders. Reflecting mainly the conditions of the sixth to the eighth centuries AD, its roots may go back to the fourth century BC, when Rhodes served as a commercial centre of world importance. They may even reach further into the eastern Mediterranean seafaring tradition of the first and second millennia BC. Codified into Roman Law, the Rhodian Sea Law lay at the basis of the medieval maritime codes of cities like Trani and Amalfi, Pisa and Ancona, which in their turn influenced the maritime codes of northern Europe, through Barcelona, Oleron and Wisby.

The outstanding feature of the Rhodian Sea Law is its co-operative nature. It indicates a seafaring community in which the boat's crew was a close-knit party, sharing responsibilities and profits. Maritime loans and charters, the liability of the ship owner, the captain and the crew, and the handling of the cargo are some of the topics dealt with, but its main concern is navigation on the high seas and the related procedures which affected life and property. The chief legacy of the code, valid to this day, is the concept of 'General Average' and its implications:

> If the Captain is deliberating about jettison, let him ask the passengers who have goods on board; and let them take a vote what is to be done. Let there be brought into contribution the goods. . . . With the captain and passengers the valuation is not to exceed a litra; with the steersman and mate, it is not to exceed half a litra; with a sailor. . . . In the same way if goods are carried away by enemies or by robbers . . . together with the belongings of sailors, these too are to come into calculation and contribute on the same principle. If there is an agreement for sharing in gain, after everything on board ship and the ship itself have been brought into contribution, let every man be liable for the loss which has occurred in proportion to his share of the gain.

General Average defines the relative liability of ship, cargo, mariners, passengers, in the case of damage. For a case to be considered for General Average, the damage has to be proved unavoidable and precalculated; there are detailed definitions of the differences between catastrophe and negligence. Contributions are calculated on the basis of purchase price, without profit.

A maritime commercial venture, more than any regular business, has

*A fifteenth-century woodcut of the port of Rhodes, the birthplace of maritime law*

always needed a large initial investment. The main legal instrument for pooling capital and bringing together investors of money and labour was the contract most often known by the medieval Italian name of *commenda*, although in other times and places it had different names, such as the Venetian *collegantia* or the Muslim *muqārada*. It held a position half-way between a loan and a partnership. Profits and risks were shared by the parties as in a partnership, but this only lasted for one venture or sea journey, and the lender was not liable to third parties. The *commenda* has sometimes been described as an agreement between a sedentary capitalist and an enterprising young man who had no capital but was willing to travel and to risk his life with the hope of gaining a fortune. However, the documentary evidence shows clearly that the roles were interchangeable, and there were many cases of poor people investing their meagre resources with a rich travelling merchant. A simple commenda contract reads as follows:

Venice, August 1073. In the name of the Lord. . . . I, Giovanni Lissado of Luprio, together with my heirs, have received in *collegantia* from you, Sevasto Orefice, son of Sir Trudimondo, and from your heirs, the amount of 200 pounds Venetian. I myself have invested 100 pounds in it. And with this capital we have acquired two shares in the ship of which Gosmiro da Molino is captain. I am under obligation to bring all of this with me in a commercial voyage [*taxegio*] to Thebes. . . . Indeed, by this agreement and understanding of ours, I promise to put to work this entire capital and to strive the best way I can. Then, if the capital is saved, we are to divide whatever profit the Lord may grant us from it by exact halves, without fraud and evil device. And whatever I can gain with those goods from any source, I am under obligation to invest all of it in this *collegantia*. And if all these goods are lost because of the sea or of hostile men, and this is proved – may this be averted – neither party ought to ask any of them from the other; if however some of them remain, in proportion as we invested so shall we share. Let this *collegantia* exist between us so long as our wills are fully agreed. But if I do not observe everything just as it is stated above, I, together with my heirs, then promise to give and to return to you and your heirs everything in the double, both capital and profit, out of my land and my house or out of anything that I am known to have in this world. Signature of the aforesaid Giovanni, who requested this instrument to be made; three witnesses and Domenico, clerk and notary, who completed and certified the instrument.

Beside the various contracts of the *commenda* type, the straight sea loan was widely used, and played a major role in maritime legislation throughout its history. Sea loans were different from regular loans in that the lender took the risk upon himself, and the borrower pledged to return his debt only upon his safe arrival. This feature elevated interest rates to anything between 10 and 100 per cent. The law made continuous attempts to limit the exorbitant interest rates, but to no avail. As insurance was non-existent, the interest had

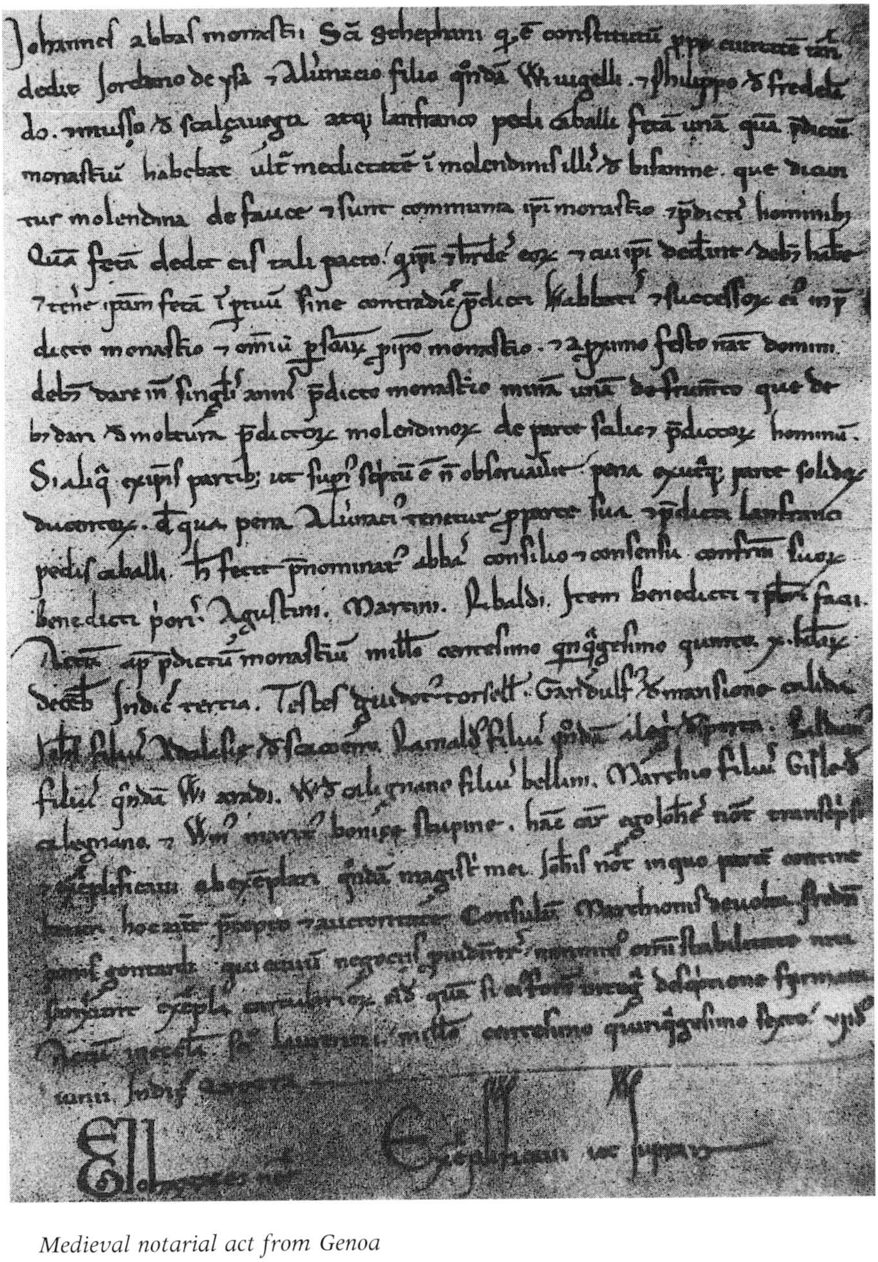

*Medieval notarial act from Genoa*

to cover the risk, which some scholars estimate as 50 per cent and more. Given this kind of deal, it is no wonder that many tried to get away when the time came to pay their dues. To prevent this, the ship or cargo, or both, served as security for the payment of the debt. Sometimes the high interest was concealed under a contract of exchange – *cambio* – as most sea loans involved the exchange of currency. In the Middle Ages, especially after the 1230s, usury was banned by the Church, even on maritime loans (where formerly interest was justified by the risk taken), so the sea exchange contracts became very popular:

> Marseille, April 2, 1227. In the name of the Lord . . . Be it known to all that I, alHakim, saracen of Alexandria, acknowledge and recognize that I have had and received, by virtue of a purchase from you, Bernard Manduel, 2 quintals of Socotran aloes and 1 quintal 80 pounds of cassia bark, and 2 centenaria of coral, for all of which I owe you 135 bezants of good alloy, old and of correct weight, waiving [all exceptions]. . . . And these 135 bezants, net of duty and of all customs, I promise by stipulation to pay fully and to deliver peacefully to you, said Bernard, or to your accredited messenger, in Ceuta within a space of twenty days after the ship 'The Falcon' arrives there. And for these I pledge to you as security all the aforesaid goods which I bought from you, and these goods are to go and remain at your risk for the said value of 135 bezants and any surplus value to be at my risk. This is to be so done that if I do not pay you the said 135 bezants by the established time limit, you are then permitted on your own authority to sell all said security . . . until you have been fully paid . . . and I also promise in good faith, under pledge of all my goods, to restore to you the whole of what may be lacking. . . . This was done in a certain house of the late Anselme, in which Januaire the notary lives. Witnesses called and invited for this purpose were Guy of Aix, Peire de Cadeilhac, etc., and I Januaire, public notary of Marseilles, by commission of both parties, wrote this.

Countless thousands of documents of this nature were preserved in the archives of maritime cities in south-western Europe from the twelfth century on. They constitute a mine of information on all aspects of maritime activity, and especially on its legal aspects. They consist of notarial instruments, such as those quoted above, as well as judicial acts, promissory notes, and samples of accounting. Official and public documents, such as port and customs records, royal and municipal regulations, and guild statutes, enter the scene a little later. A third important source is merchants' private correspondence, manuals and treatises on commerce and affiliated topics. These treasures are far from being exhausted; they are just beginning to be catalogued.

It is interesting to note that in the document cited above, the loan is contracted between a Muslim and a Christian at the height of the crusading period. According to Muslim Law,

> there is nothing wrong with a Moslem accepting a capital from a Christian as a *commenda*, since doing this is a category of trade and of commercial activity. . . . There is nothing wrong with a Moslem overseeing sales and purchases on behalf of a Christian as his agent. . . . Even though it is judicially permissible, it is reprehensible for a Moslem to entrust capital as a *commenda* to a Christian, just as it is reprehensible for a Moslem to mandate a Christian to work with his capital. This is so, because in the latter case the person directly overseeing the transactions is the Christian, who will not guard against usury, nor will he be aware of the factors which invalidate the contract, nor will he, because of his faith, guard against them. Similarly, he will deal in wine and pork, and it is reprehensible for a Moslem to deputize another person to deal in these commodities.

During the fourteenth century, it became rare for merchants to travel with their wares, as trading centres were developing and commerce was conducted on an increasingly large scale. Banks and big merchant firms looked after the financing, while agents dealt with the routine business, working on commission or on a salary. Double-entry bookkeeping was introduced, and the true insurance contract was developed, with underwriting companies specializing in this branch of finance. Even the nucleus of the future share-holding companies existed in the Mediterranean at the end of the Middle Ages, as in the Genoese Maona of Chios or Cyprus. Although most of these techniques were used over land as well, and the big fairs contributed much to the development of commerce, it was maritime trade which was at the basis of these systems and used them to a much higher degree. By the sixteenth century, the modern era had a firm basis on which to carry on its world-wide commercial network.

In the trading centres which were established overseas during the commercial revolution of the twelfth and thirteenth centuries AD, in close conjunction with the crusading movement, the special legal status of foreign merchants was broadened to establish an extra-territorial entity, anchored in international agreements. The origin of these agreements lay in the privileges accorded to the mother cities under special circumstances; they were, for instance, rewarded for assistance given in times of war. The status given to the Italian Communities in the crusader kingdom of Jerusalem was an important turning point. Following the conquest of Tyre in 1123, Venice received the following privileges:

– The authorities are responsible for the safety of the Venetians coming into the country to trade and for their property.

– The Venetians are exempt from all taxes and dues, except for those on the transport of pilgrims.

– In every town of the kingdom, the Venetians will have their own quarter, including a main street, a marketplace, a church, a bath-house, a mill, a bakery, all of which they will own, free of any charge.

– They may use their own weights and measures when dealing among themselves and when selling to others; when buying, they should use the King's measures.

– The Venetians will have their own courts to judge their citizens, except when the party sued is not Venetian.

– They will also have authority over the population resident in their quarter.

– When a Venetian dies intestate, his property will revert to the Venetian community.

– Venetian life and property salvaged from shipwreck will be handed over to the Venetian community.

Other commercial towns received similar concessions before and after this famous Pactum Warmundi (called after the patriarch who signed it). Their impact was carried into the twentieth century through the Ottoman capitulations (so called after their paragraphs, *capituli*) – commercial treaties – which were modelled after them. These trading centres were run by the consuls mentioned above, and their physical features still dot the Mediterranean coastal landscape. 'Lombard Street' in many a western European town, the residence of north Italian merchants, was the financial and international commercial focus of economic life; the Fondaco dei Tedeschi in Venice (today's central Post Office by the Rialto Bridge) was the lodge of the German merchants, who came down the Alps to sell their products and buy fancy eastern imports; the Galata suburb of Istanbul was originally a Genoese trading colony in the Byzantine Empire; Khan el Ifrang in Acre was the Venetian *fondaco*, turned over to the French merchants by the Ottomans, and now serving as a high school run by the Franciscan Order.

Besides the precepts guiding commercial contracts and the agreements governing merchant colonies, a whole range of regulations pertaining to navigation had existed since early times. They dealt with the time of sailing, with its mode (convoys, line and tramp shipping), and with security on board. The rules listing the obligatory gear and equipment and the loading procedures are very detailed; they include the marking of the load-line for different types of voyage, of ship and of cargo. Chartering contracts specified, just as they do today, the duration of the venture, its scope, the crew and its duties, the gear and equipment included, as well as the obligations on the part of the users and the terms of payment. A typical bill of lading from twelfth-century Egypt reads as follows:

O God, in your mercy grant safety for Joseph, son of Khalfa . . ., to a bundle containing 32 Tripolitanian cloaks; 2 red cloaks; 2 hides serving as covers; 40 Sicilian cloths wrapped in a washed mantle; 4 boxes of saffron; 5 Sicilian cloths, a turban made of cotton. All are wrapped in underpants. May God decree safety for it. Amen. . . .

Although concepts like the right of innocent passage or the economic war of attrition have existed since time immemorial, the law governing war at sea is a relatively new creation. Most of the legislation in this field originated outside the Mediterranean. The Dutch Hugo Grotius (Huig de Groot, 1583–1645), eager to defend his country's rights against British domination and the concept of 'closed seas', is credited with the first modern definition of the freedom of the seas. His philosophy was highly important, but of much more immediate application were the English rules against piracy. Until the nineteenth century, most states endorsed privateering, as long as it matched their political and economic interests. Laws against piracy were enacted only against those who attacked their co-citizens or co-religionists. The first country to promulgate such laws was Britain in 1536, and after that there were many amendments, until in 1824 Britain condemned all slavery, without difference of race or religion, and by doing so dealt a death blow to piracy as well. The British Admiralty regulations concerning war prizes, salvage and refugees are the foundation of the modern treatment of these

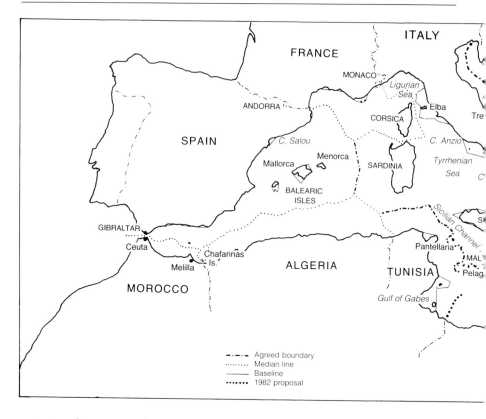

*Projected maritime political boundaries of the Mediterranean today*

topics. In spite of these major contributions, the essence of maritime law was a Mediterranean product, a complex expression of the vicissitudes of its maritime civilization.

As is evident, it is difficult to distinguish clearly between private, national and international law, especially in maritime law, where personal issues become international concerns. The first codes dealt with private matters; the city codes added regulations of a public nature, which were widened further by subsequent national codes. In the twentieth century, these codes are being incorporated into a common international law (see Appendix C).

The Mediterranean, because of its special physical nature and political circumstances, poses additional problems, which call for particular consideration. Few Mediterranean countries may claim the 200 mile Exclusive

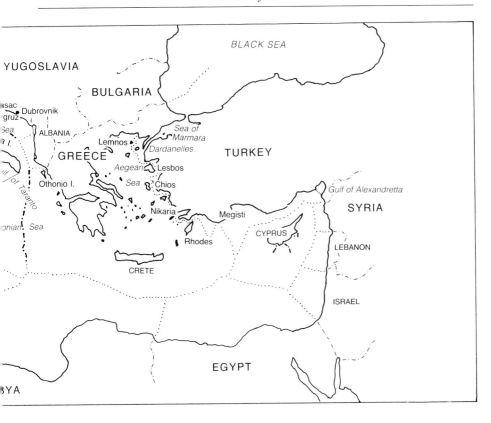

Economic Zone, for instance, or the continental margin, two important issues
in the new law of the sea. Three of the most sensitive straits in the world are
located in it, and its inner seas, dotted with islands, make the drawing of
boundaries extremely difficult. While some of the disputes are historical,
others pertain to new areas of interest, such as the sea bottom. The prospects
of finding resources and the technical development of submarine craft and
warheads bear heavily on the amount of pressure evident in these disputes.
The sciences of geology, oceanography and cartography, side by side with
military strategy, play a decisive role in settling the issues. Reconnaissance in
this new struggle is carried out as much by the scientists as by the military; in
fact, the former sometimes seems to be more mysterious than the secret
services. Scientific papers held in safe deposits are not very helpful for the
development of science, but do demonstrate the high regard in which science
is held in this era of accelerated progress.

Following the 1982 convention (see p. 121), countries with an indented coastline or with offshore islands under their rule, could proclaim straight baselines (imaginary lines drawn along irregular coastlines from which various zones can be determined) and closed gulfs, on which to base their territorial water claims. Several Mediterranean countries have done so; their cases are still being debated. One important issue is the division of the continental shelf between Tunisia and Libya, because of its potential in natural resources. Here the Kerkenna Islands are the bone of contention, while the Isole Pelagie pose the same problem in the Sicilian Channel. A dispute between Malta and Libya concerns the nature of the continental shelf between them – the Medina Bank, an isolated mound in a submarine valley – which both of them claim. In the Aegean, Turkey claims its share of sea on a demographic basis (eight million Turks live on the eastern coast) and not of area (a total of half a million Greeks inhabit all the islands, in an area of more than 5,000 square kilometres); there are problematic areas around Gibraltar (disputed between Spain and Britain) and Cyprus (divided between Greece and Turkey). Libya's claim to the Gulf of Sirta (Sydra) has created another high-tension zone. This crowded and depressing picture is brightened up by other developments, such as the agreements reached between Italy and four of its neighbours. The principle of equidistance could not apply, so there were outstanding concessions, on the part of Yugoslavia, for instance. These are the first maritime boundaries agreed upon in the Mediterranean, and may serve as an example in other similar situations, where international legal agreement may foreclose the prospect of war.

CHAPTER 10

# THEATRE OF WAR

T HE MEDITERRANEAN could be the sea of the highest strategic
importance in the world today. It contains the home bases of the
eighteen Mediterranean countries, and fleets of the major world powers in
ever-increasing numbers – the biggest concentration of naval units to be
found anywhere in the world: 'Like frogs around a pond we have settled
down upon the shores of this sea' – this much-quoted passage from Plato's
*Phaedo* is still very true. In this deep body of water, with its complex
contours, all kinds of vessels swarm – on the surface and below. Their main
purpose is defensive and deterrent; patrols to keep the sea-lanes free, a
military presence to prevent any hostile offensive. This very concentration is
dangerous in itself, threatening not merely a conventional type of war, but
even a nuclear one. There are thoughts of making the entire sea neutral, but at
present these are utopian.

Command of the sea can easily be secured in the Mediterranean by the
seizure of strategic points along the sea-routes, which indeed were the sites of
the major naval engagements in previous centuries. Throughout its long
history, naval warfare in the Mediterranean constituted an inseparable part
of the history of its people. No single power in antiquity was able to secure
complete mastery of the whole basin, except the Roman Empire in its heyday.
In fact the Mediterranean was divided, over and over again, after protracted
and costly wars, between pairs of competing powers – the Greeks and the
Phoenicians, Byzantium and Islam, Venice and Genoa, Spain and the Turks.
In retrospect, we may even discern some constants which reappear
throughout its history in different circumstances. Today both the USA and
the USSR, with their respective alliances, as well as Great Britain, maintain
bases and training areas in different parts of the sea, mainly on the islands, for
example Cyprus and Crete, Sicily and the Balearics, the same spots that
served earlier maritime powers.

Before the modern era, neither the Atlantic nor the Pacific had any special

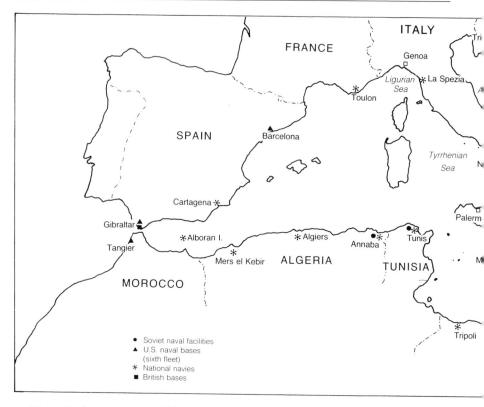

*Major Mediterranean naval bases*

kind of warship, let alone naval squadrons; seafaring seems to have developed independently in all the oceans, but proper naval warfare was introduced into them from the Mediterranean which, with its unique geo-political features, formed an arena for the development of warfare at sea on parallel lines with the art of war on land.

For 3,000 years the oared vessel carried the main burden of Mediterranean naval warfare. It is amazing how little this ship changed during these millennia. As early as the second millennium BC, its main features were apparent: it was long and narrow, and carried a large, well-trained contingent of oarsmen, together with an auxiliary sail for long voyages. At first, there was just one set of oars, but later on, a second was added, and the vessel became a bireme. The three-oar system of the trireme, developed by

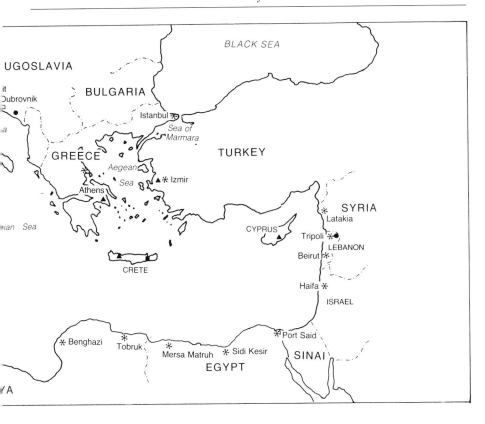

the Greeks around 700 BC, proved to be the optimum, but the sources tell us also of quadriremes and quinqueremes. These were multiplications of the average twenty-five oars to the side, giving about a hundred oars for the bireme and a hundred and fifty for the trireme. Even with the rowers arranged on different levels, it is difficult to imagine how the oars could be co-ordinated, and the length and weight of the upper oars.

Most of our information concerning these boats is derived from textual and artistic sources. This type of boat, when wrecked, disintegrated and disappeared entirely. This accounts for the heated discussions about the structure of ancient battlecraft, culminating in various theories that are held about the arrangement of the oars. A unique experiment, which is taking place in Greece under the guidance of English scholars, is attempting to solve this problem once and for all. In 1987, a *trieres* (or trireme) was launched in Piraeus, amid great festivities. It was reconstructed from literary and iconographic sources such as vase-paintings, reliefs and coins, in a Greek shipyard near Piraeus, with the co-operation of the Hellenic navy. Until a well-preserved classical warship is discovered by marine archaeologists this is the best means we have of understanding these vessels. The *Olympias* is 37 m long, 6 m at the beam, with a shallow draught of about 2m. The crew consists of 170 rowers, seated on three levels, who have to manoeuvre in perfect unison in order to realize the full potential of the boat. In 1860, Napoleon III tried the same feat and failed miserably (for similar trials see Chapter 4).

One of the most famous sea battles in history and a crucial one for the Greek world was fought by several hundreds of these triremes at Salamis in 480 BC. The Persian army, with its Phoenician allies, advanced from the East on both land and sea, and was about to conquer the whole of Greece. The Athenians made a desperate move, unprecedented hitherto – they abandoned their city and staked everything on the outcome of the battle, which they won in spite of their inferior numbers. The Persian ships were crowded in the small bay, and the Greeks exercised their disciplined tactics perfectly, taking advantage of the wind and local conditions. Even for modern Greeks, fighting for their independence, Salamis became the symbol of civilization's triumph over the 'barbarians'.

The Romans reverted to the bireme, which they called *liburnia*, after an Illyric boat. The Byzantine *dromon* (swift) was an adaptation of this same model. In the medieval warship, called a galley (*galea, gallera*, first mentioned in the ninth century), all rowers were seated on one level, using an outrigger (a lateral projection above the waterline), which supported about twenty-five pairs of oars to the side, later turned into groups of three. The last model in this long line of development was the galiasse, a vessel of over 200 tonnes, rowed by more than 200 *galeoti* and carrying about as many armoured fighters. On the galiasse, the groups of three oars were amalgamated into one oar per bank. The oars grew to huge proportions, carried a heavy weight on their inner part for balance and were manned by up to five men each. These boats were extremely crowded, and battle engagements inflicted a great loss of life. Originally, the oarsmen were free citizens, in Venice as in ancient Greece. At the end of the Middle Ages, when it became increasingly difficult to recruit the manpower needed, the authorities started using prisoners of war and convicts to man their war fleets. Those days are over, and now free young men relive the exhilarating experience of solidarity, speed and manoeuvrability in countless rowing races, among them the Venetian regattas, the topic of famous paintings and a very picturesque sight. The last

*Greek warships as depicted on a sixth-century BC vase*

great galleys and galiasses of the Mediterranean, dating from the sixteenth century, are displayed in the museums of Venice, Barcelona and Istanbul.

It took more than a century after the introduction of firearms on board ship and the perfection of the rigging, for the fighting sailing ships to take over, and for the oared galleys to be finally phased out: this occurred at the end of the sixteenth century. However, because of their long and powerful tradition, galleys were still being built in the Mediterranean and elsewhere well into the eighteenth century. Peter the Great of Russia had them built in the Baltic at the end of the seventeenth century, with the help of Dutch shipwrights.

One of the biggest advantages of the galleys which gave them another lease of life was their lightness, making them easy to carry and beach. History tells many stories of surprise attacks by galleys built in a defended dockyard or arsenal, which were carried overland to the site of battle, quickly assembled and launched, to take the enemy completely by surprise. One famous case is the attack on Mecca with ships built in Krak, Transjordan, by the daring crusader Reinaud de Chatillon. In 1439, the Venetians fought the Milanese on Lago di Garda with ships built across the mountains. Unfortunately, some of them sank, thus becoming the oldest specimens of this kind of boat yet discovered from the Mediterranean region.

The ultimate goal of naval warfare is the destruction of the enemy's force, the annihilation of the ships themselves. Modern tactics are based on long-range hits by super warheads, but in antiquity sinking an enemy ship was a difficult task, and was usually discarded in favour of boarding and hand-to-hand fighting. But for several centuries this method was replaced by a direct one – the practice of ramming, which turned the ship itself into the decisive weapon. The ramming manoeuvre required the highest degree of skill and discipline, and was perfected mainly in classical Greece, after which it declined rapidly. Ramming was the culmination of naval tactics. In Marsala, western Sicily, two Punic vessels with long wooden beaks have been excavated by the English marine archaeologist Honor Frost, who claims they are typical warships. In Athlit, Israel, a rare discovery threw unexpected light on this phase of naval warfare: a three-pronged bronze ram of the Hellenistic period, weighing about half a tonne, was discovered in 1980, with part of the prow carrying it. The ram is beautifully decorated on both sides with symbols of power and seaworthiness: an eagle's head, the helmet and star of the Dioscuri, and the trident. The Israeli Elisha Linder has led an international team in the study of this ram; this study has implications in several related fields, such as ancient metallurgy, shipbuilding and iconography.

The Romans, essentially a continental power, tried to fight land battles at sea. They relied on the *corvus*, the boarding bridge, a cumbersome piece of equipment mounted on the prow, which dropped on the enemy ship and enabled the Roman legionnaires-turned-marines to storm over it. In a decisive battle against their major rival, the Punic maritime empire centred around Carthage (Tunis), the Romans in 241 BC managed to manoeuvre their enemies into the perfect situation for boarding. Near the Egadi islands, off the north-western tip of Sicily, hundreds of Punic ships were sunk or captured through boarding, thus ending the first Punic war; Rome had the upper hand and was recognized as a superior sea power. The last and most famous of Roman sea battles was Actium (at the entrance of the Bay of Corinth), fought in 31 BC. The navies on both sides comprised hundreds of vessels, and included the towering monsters, quadriremes and quinqueremes. There was no room for a true engagement, and the battle was decided at long range. Antony and Cleopatra fled and later committed suicide, while the Caesar

Octavian returned to Rome to start a new age of unchallenged Roman rule over the entire Mediterranean.

The tactics of land battle at sea were adopted by the Muslims when they first ventured on the water, for the same reasons. Only one generation after coming out of the desert, the nascent Muslim navy defeated its glorious Byzantine opponent in the 'Battle of the Masts', fought off the coasts of Cilicia (Turkey) in 655. Victory was achieved by chaining the boats together to form a fighting platform, and using grapnels and hooks on the enemy ships. After this victory, the Muslims proceeded to put the Byzantine capital itself under siege. During that siege a new weapon was used, which was said to have driven the Muslims to abandon their plans. The so-called 'Greek fire', an inflammable substance thrown on the enemy ship through syphons or by clay containers, was an important move in the direction of long-range fighting. The secret of the concoction (said to have been invented in Syracuse in the fourth century BC), which caught fire when it touched the water, is still not wholly understood. It is thought to be made of crude oil, naphtha or bitumen, sulphur, quicklime and saltpetre or potash. But Greek fire was lethal to both sides, and soon became confined to maritime sieges. An efficient siege was a major problem for the oared fighting craft, for they had no room for storage and no sleeping quarters, and indeed needed a base in which to spend the nights. The near impossibility of a naval siege was one of the factors of the political independence of coastal towns down to modern times.

During the Greek War of Independence in the 1820s, much use was made of another form of fire, the fire ship. It consisted of an old boat, loaded with ammunition, which was secretly towed out to the enemy ships, hooked to them and ignited. The attacking party would then quickly withdraw in a small boat. The appearance of steel ships soon made this technique obsolete, demanding instead torpedoes and other lethal innovations. Indeed, at the same time as this archaic form of naval warfare was being used, a British steam warship made its debut.

At the end of the Middle Ages, the general tendency in naval warfare was the move to projectile weapons, such as crossbows (arbalests), on board ship. The introduction of guns, which followed soon after, caused far-reaching changes. Although initially clumsy and inefficient, and quite ineffective in traditional tactics, they finally prevailed and created a new naval reality. The oared fighting ship, unfit to carry a great number of guns, finally disappeared from the scene, after thousands of years of active service. In the fifteenth and sixteenth centuries there were many battles, in the Mediterranean and in the Atlantic, in which oared galleys and gunships under sail fought each other.

The galleys were more vulnerable, but the sailing ships were wholly dependent on the wind and heavy to manoeuvre under the weight of their guns. The guns themselves, breech-loading, had a six-foot recoil, and had to be tied by ropes to their positions. Even so, there were many casualties among their fourteen-man crews. Their range was limited and accuracy minimal, while the intervals between shots rendered them almost useless.

One of the last battles of the oared galleys was fought in 1571, at Lepanto, in the Gulf of Patras in western Greece. The Christian Holy League commanded by Don Juan of Austria had over 200 galleys, mainly Venetian, and the Ottoman Turks had a slightly larger number. The losses on the Turkish side were 30,000 men and over 150 ships, on the Christian side 9,000 dead and twelve galleys lost. Despite the great Christian victory, nobody won that war, and seventeen years later, with the defeat of the great Spanish Armada, the galleys finally lost the battle. Four hundred years later, the site of the Battle of Lepanto was revisited by scientists, headed by Harold Edgerton who experimented with his newly invented sonar equipment, in an attempt to find the remains of the long sought-after Mediterranean battleship.

In sea battles, one key to victory was the separation of the oared warships from the slower escort, which was dependent on sail alone; this was similar to a common strategy in land battles, where mounted fighters were separated from the foot-soldiers and the baggage train. Many types of 'cross breeds' were designed to overcome this problem, combining oars and sails, the speed of the warship with the capacity of the general carrier. These types of boats were favoured particularly by the pirates, who were endemic to the Mediterranean from time immemorial until the beginning of our century.

Piracy flourished when command of the sea was weak or disputed, and when maritime trade was not well established or was declining. Command of the sea could then be challenged by guerrilla warfare, in which case the pirates were considered licensed privateers, or corsairs. An inscription from the island of Samos, from around 500 BC, immortalized a blessing given to the pirates by the local government and the gods.

Commercial transactions in valuables like spices, slaves and other luxury items such as precious metals and currency lured the pirates, who would hunt down their prey. In Mediterranean history, there were several important centres which constantly served as pirates' nests: Crete, Rhodes, Cilicia and the Dalmatian coast in the eastern Mediterranean, Malta, Algiers, Corsica and the Balearics in the western basin. It seemed that whoever settled in these areas would sooner or later turn to piracy or privateering.

Ancient piracy came to a standstill after Pompey's campaign of 67 BC. In a well co-ordinated effort that lasted three months, using twenty legions (about 120,000 men) and close to 500 ships, he fell upon all the major pirate nests at once, then dealt them the final blow in their last stronghold at Coracesion, in southern Anatolia. Plutarch tells us that he captured more than a thousand pirate ships and subdued 400 of their cities, with tens of thousands of men imprisoned and enslaved. This campaign freed the Mediterranean of a serious piratical menace for centuries.

In the Middle Ages, the scourge of piracy was at its worst. After the depredations of the Vandals, the Muslims used Tunisia as the main base for their piratical raids on Christendom. During the ninth century, most Mediterranean islands were conquered by Muslim forces, with bridgeheads on the mainland, at Thasos (opposite Saloniki), Bari in the spur of Italy and La Garde Fraînet in the French Massif des Maures. The wars of religion culminating with the Crusades gave licence to piratical raids on both sides. These were sanctioned as holy, although the pirates often did not distinguish among their victims. Even the churches accepted the booty as a legitimate donation; patron saints and religious institutions were given their share of the profits as a matter of course. In the early modern age, Mediterranean piracy declined, while the corsairs, authorized pirates, reached new heights of activity and general recognition.

Malta became the headquarters of the Order of St John, pirate monks who started their history as the Knights Hospitallers in the crusader kingdom of Jerusalem. After its fall, they specialized in fighting the infidel by piratical raids from their consecutive strongholds in Cyprus, Rhodes and Malta. There is a strange connection between the Knights of Malta and the Russian entry into Mediterranean naval affairs. After Napoleon drove the Knights out of Malta, the Tsar Paul I, who had previously become Grand Master of the Order, decided to launch a crusade against the French Egyptian campaign. From then on, the Russian presence in the Mediterranean has been almost uninterrupted. In fact, the first Russian naval action in the Mediterranean had occurred about thirty years earlier, with a squadron coming from the Baltic through the Straits of Gibraltar, defeating the Turks at Chesme (Aegean Turkey) in 1770.

The case of the Barbary corsairs is another medieval story carried into the nineteenth century, which in its turn had an impact on the formation of the American navy. In the first half of the sixteenth century, the expanding Ottoman Empire enjoyed the services of a number of first-rate sea captains; two converted Greeks, the brothers Barbarossa from Lesbos (Khizr and Aruj), a converted Jew (Sinan Pasha), and the cartographer Piri Reis, all of them corsairs who were promoted to the rank of admiral (*Reis*). Some eventually became governors of provinces such as Algiers. In the seventeenth century, Algiers developed into a true pirate state, with its Beys controlling a fleet estimated at 1,500 ships and issuing their own *patentes de corso*. It is estimated that over 20,000 people engaged in piracy in the Magreb during this period; hundreds of ships were captured, thousands of people sold into slavery and the booty ran into millions. Most European nations had to compromise and sign treaties with the Barbary corsairs, actually paying them protection money, as well as buying their booty and even selling them ammunition.

After the American War of Independence, the British treaties no longer covered American trade and it suffered heavily from piratical attacks. In 1797 the first three frigates of the American navy were built for the purpose of fighting the Barbary corsairs, and in 1815 dealt them a heavy blow. Soon afterwards, the American fleet started using La Spezia as its main Mediterranean base, as it still does to this day. The French occupation of Algeria in 1830 ended piracy off that coast.

The pirates used to camouflage themselves and their boats, using false flags, women's clothes, foreign boats or boats painted blue-grey, to blend with the sea. A well-known pirate trick was forcing their prisoners to drink seawater, which made them reveal the jewels they had swallowed. This story is told by Marco Polo of the oriental pirates, but the practice was universal. Their main weapon was the surprise attack. Big ships could resist them, but average-sized single ones usually surrendered. This was the reason for the convoy system, prevalent in Mediterranean shipping up to modern times.

A special form of piracy was by 'letters of marque', or what the Italians called *represaglie*. This was an authorization to achieve a private vengeance or reparation. Intentional wrecking was a common piratical practice. By false signals, the pirates would lure a boat to a rocky beach, and plunder it after it had foundered. People were usually held for ransom, but after the banning of piracy by international law, victims were killed in order to eliminate witnesses; their ship could then be claimed as 'an abandoned wreck'.

Piracy had a devastating effect on Mediterranean life in past centuries. Whole islands were deserted and coasts abandoned, some of them remaining desolate to the present. The population moved inland, uphill behind the coast. Pirates were so strongly hated that the usual penalty meted out to them was death by fire or stoning. Both piracy and privateering played an important role in the development of the international law of the sea. As long as they were part of the system, with respectable ports of call which traded in their goods, nothing could be done. But once the concept of the freedom of the seas was accepted, the way was open for its implementation. In Paris 1856, all European countries signed a declaration banning all forms of piracy and privateering, and the new armed steam ship, which appeared just at that moment, easily enforced the ban.

Returning to early modern times, the development of the gunship is the most outstanding feature of naval warfare. Even before Lepanto, at the beginning of the sixteenth century, the French had the original idea of piercing the sides of their ships in order to put guns below deck. In the following century, sailing ships were converted to carry as many guns as possible, turning into purely fighting ships quite different from the trading vessels. From then on, warships were classified not according to the number of the oars, but as carrying so many guns. A first-rate ship had more than a hundred guns on board, mostly on three decks, with the heaviest guns on the lower deck and the light ones on the upper. A sixth-rate ship had twenty to thirty guns, and few carried less. An especially popular gun aboard ship was the culverin; the shot was varied, from stone and iron balls to special exploding devices.

The gun batteries on the ship's sides had a deep impact on naval tactics. Since antiquity, many theories of *naumachia* or naval warfare had been put forward. Essentially, however, the tactics were quite simple; flanking or breaking through. These were achieved with two basic formations – the line abreast and the crescent shape. The new sailing gunship introduced a different basic formation, the 'line ahead' system, hence the term 'ship of the line'. The position for attack was no longer with the prow ahead, to use the ram or landing bridge, but sideways, for maximum gunpower. Paradoxically, the wind continued to have a major role in sea battles, for high waves would put the lowest, heaviest guns out of action.

Following three centuries of empire building, while most decisive sea battles were fought far away from the Mediterranean, the nineteenth century again brought the Mediterranean into the focus of international affairs. The English–French struggle, the 'Sick Man of the Bosporus' and the rising power of Russia, the Greek and Italian Wars of Independence, resulted in intensive naval activity all over the Mediterranean, with many a sea battle which became the core of legend and national pride. The Napoleonic campaigns and the great naval battles of the nineteenth century left the sea-bed littered with naval cannon, some of which were sunk on purpose, to avoid their falling into enemy hands. Most of the guns of that period which have survived were retrieved from the sea, as those found on land were usually recast to make new ones. Guns dating to the end of the eighteenth century were recovered off the Israeli coast at Dor. After his failure to capture Acre in 1799, Napoleon dumped them into the sea in order to make his retreat easier. Some of them were Turkish guns, previously taken as booty.

Even during the Second World War, when navies were engaged in the Atlantic and the Pacific, the Mediterranean still remained the hub of activity, with coastal strips and islands suffering heavy loss and damage. The outstanding naval engagements in recent history are, with hardly an exception, re-enactments of older battles in the very same places. In the Turkish straits, Troy and Gallipoli are the two most famous sites. During the First World War, one of the most tragic events in the history of mankind was staged in Gallipoli. In 1915, Britain decided to open an eastern supply route to Russia, but this strategically brilliant idea was compromised by tactical weakness – warships alone could not reduce the strong coastal fortifications, the new underwater minefields were terribly effective, and the amphibious assault lacked co-ordination, specialized techniques and equipment. From April 1915 until complete withdrawal in January 1916, a force of 80,000 men was almost annihilated, and many of the heroic 30,000 Turkish defenders were killed too. The cemeteries in Gallipoli seem to stretch forever, a silent testimony to the limits of strategic theory. As for Troy, had the traditions of the other side survived, beside those of the victorious Greeks, we would probably have had another story of calamity and destruction. At Abidos, between Troy and Gallipoli, a less well-known war was fought at the beginning of the fourteenth century, between the two leading maritime empires of the time – Genoa and Venice.

The western bays separating mainland Greece from the Peloponnese were the site of several decisive sea battles: Octavian defeated Antony and Cleopatra at Actium in 31 BC, a general rehearsal for Lepanto was carried out between Turks and Christians at Preveza in 1538, and thirty-three years later, the Battle of Lepanto took place in that same area; at Navarino in 1827, British and French forces changed the course of the Greek War of Independence. In the isthmus of Suez, another highly sensitive area, the site of Abou-Kir, Nelson's great victory over Napoleon, is adjacent to Damietta, where another French monarch, St Louis, was badly defeated and humiliated on his crusade of 1249–50. The Sinai campaign of 1956 was fought around the Suez Canal as well. Finally, the straits of Sicily were the scene of many a decisive sea battle; the island of Malta was besieged time and again, by the Turks in 1565 and by the Germans in 1941. It stood heroically during both

Jeanne d'Arc, *a helicopter carrier*

these ordeals, a source of national pride and pageantry.

The introduction of submarine and aerial raids into naval warfare brought about a major change in strategy and tactics. After the Second World War, the all-pervading line-ahead formation was abandoned, together with the 'ship of the line', in favour of a close defensive formation, with the aircraft carriers and other essential ships protected on all sides by gun and torpedo boats. This is reminiscent of an old, classical Greek naval strategy (obsolete since the disappearance of the triremes and ramming tactics) called the *kiklos* – a circular formation by which all warships turned their prows outward.

The crucial activities of the naval elite units, the so-called 'frogmen' of underwater commandos, can be seen as another revival of archaic practices. The story of the Italian submarine *Scire* and its special force is symbolic of the pioneering and heroic role of frogmen in modern naval warfare. During the Second World War, the Italians built a torpedo-like mini-sub, attached to the body of the main submarine craft, from which underwater commando fighters could perform special tasks. The *Scire* carried three such 'pigs' and during 1942 inflicted heavy losses on the British in the waters of the Levant, its divers excelling in courage and ingenuity. It was sunk that year in the Bay of Haifa, where it was discovered in the 1960s, lying almost intact under 33 m of water. After they despaired of surfacing her, the Italian authorities declared the site a communal grave, and there she stayed, with about forty men and live ammunition still on board.

One thing is certain – the removal of the naval bases dotting this sea would open up possibilities for the further exploration of innumerable sites, some of them among the most ancient and enchanting in the Mediterranean, to research and tourism – Alexandria and Athlit, Gaeta and Cadiz. But in our own post-war oil era, tension around the Mediterranean is constant; one crisis follows another with the successive wars between Israel and the Arab countries, the skirmishes of Libya with the US, and the growing terrorist menace on land, air and sea. It seems as if piracy and privateering are back in full force, and violence at sea is raising its monstrous head again. Since the Arab–Israeli war of 1973, dozens of terrorist acts have been carried out in the Middle East against ships from all over the world, most of them general carriers, with a great loss of life and property.

Should history be left to take its own course, or will people come to their senses, and unified mankind arise to prevent the sword of doom from menacing this crowded centre of culture and civilization?

*A 17,500-tonne luxury cruise hotel plying the Mediterranean*

*The Greek archipelago (seen from Delos), a bone of contention to this day*

*A Greek trireme, reconstructed and launched in 1987*

*Raising a seventeenth-century naval gun from the seabed in Israel*

*The three-pronged Hellenistic ram of Athlit*

*The Battle of Preveza 1538, precursor of Lepanto*

*Kotor in Yugoslavia, a natural pirates' nest*

*A fresco from Akrotiri, on the island of Thera*

*The temple of Apollo in Corinth, Greece*

*The Norman Capella Palatina in Palermo, Sicily: Muslim woodwork on the ceiling and Byzantine mosaics*

*The Muslim fortress on the Roman theatre of Malaga, Spain*

*'The Sposalizio' by Canaletto*

*The fortress-church of Les Stes. Maries-de-la-Mer, Provence*

*'Portrait de Jeune Fille' by Pablo Picasso*

CHAPTER 11

# WAVES OF MIGRATION

E VERY YEAR from May to October, millions of northern Europeans, as
well as Americans and Orientals, crowd the Mediterranean shores, to a
point where a naive onlooker might fear that the continent might tilt. Some,
like their Germanic and Viking ancestors, are drawn to the richness and
warmth of the southern coasts. For others the Mediterranean is the cradle of
civilization, the birthplace of monotheistic religion, the source of western
culture. Yet others are looking for crowded or deserted beaches, and for
landscapes which are familiar yet ever-changing. Although tourism constitutes an important part of the budget of several Mediterranean countries, life
outside the tourist resorts goes on almost unaffected. Old languages and
dialects are spoken; English is only superficially known. The peculiar
Mediterranean rhythm of lazy action and long hours of rest, strange meal
times, closed or unmanned offices, inefficient communications – in short, the
notorious Mediterranean life-style – still lingers on. On the other hand, a
genuinely humane touch permeates life. Women may be discriminated
against, but they are adored and treated in a way not found anywhere else.
Everybody's joy and sorrow are shared by all, and Mediterranean
hospitality, especially in the Muslim countries, is proverbial. What are the
roots of this heritage and its common features?

Prehistoric research has shown that man lived around the Mediterranean
through the Ice Age, when there were just channels separating Europe from
Africa and the islands were easy to reach. The fourth millennium BC or the
Chalcolithic Age was a period of intense activity. In the third millennium
islands were settled, cities developed, and the first dynasties of rulers
established the two oldest states in world history, in the river valleys of
Egypt and Mesopotamia. In fact, history itself begins then, with written
records added to the material remains which had previously served as sole
evidence of these developments.

The Egyptian and Mesopotamian Empires had their ups and downs, and in the second millennium BC were joined by a third power in Anatolia – the Hittites. These people were one of a long line of Asiatic invaders, who settled around the Mediterranean, adopted its common culture and in their turn deeply influenced its character. The Hittites were a typical land power. They were so averse to the sea that scholars have attributed to them a measure of *thalassophobia*. To the west, mainly in the Aegean archipelago, the Minoans and Myceneans held sway, basing their power on sea trade and communications, thus constituting the first thalassocracies. The fourteenth century BC stands out as an early peak in Mediterranean cultural history. It is the 'ElAmarna Age', so called after the new capital of the eighteenth Egyptian dynasty. This period is known first for its Pharaoh Amenhotep IV 'Akhenaton', who is considered the father of monotheism, secondly for his heir Tut-Ankh-Amon, whose tomb was discovered undisturbed, and thirdly for the ElAmarna archives. The historian and philologist Cyrus H. Gordon regards this period as the common background to Hebrew and Greek civilizations. According to him, the eastern Mediterranean basin constituted at that time a true *oecumene* – Greek for the whole civilized world, beyond which there are the 'barbarians'.

The 1200s were the end of an era. The Egyptian, Hittite and Mycenean Empires crumbled, and Bronze Age civilization waned. These years are a 'black hole' in Mediterranean history. An enormous wave of sea nomads swept over the eastern Mediterranean shores. These 'Sea People', whose origin is now thought to be the Aegean orbit, launched the first known large-scale immigration by sea. The famous sea battle of the Pharaoh Ramses II against them (1189 BC) drew on the naval traditions of the ElAmarna Age. It saved the Nile delta from deep penetration, but the Sea People settled (sometimes through an Egyptian initiative) along the Syro-Palestinian coast. Its southern part got its name from some of these people, the Palashtu (Philistines), who are mentioned in the Bible as the foes of Samson, Saul and David. Other Sea People settled in the islands to the west, to which they gave their names – Crete and Sicily (which were both referred to as Tjekker or Shiqalaya), and Sardinia (Sherden).

Out of this chaos rose the new thalassocracy of the Phoenicians. Their cities occupied the centre of the triangle made up of the wealthiest countries of the then known world – Egypt, Mesopotamia and Anatolia. They took full advantage of this fact, and by the tenth century started to expand to the west. The Greeks first welcomed them, as what they had to offer was far superior to anything archaic Greece knew and made at the time. During the eighth and seventh centuries BC, the confrontation between Shem and Japheth grew

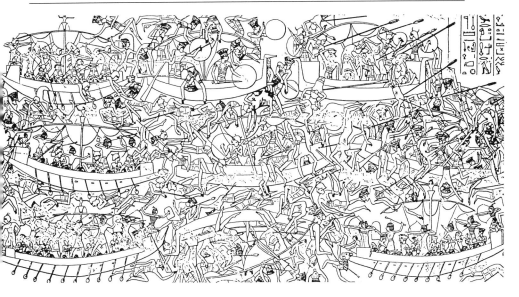

*The Sea People in a naval battle with the Egyptians, c. 1200 BC*

fierce, as Greek colonization pushed into Phoenician spheres of influence in the Black Sea, Italy and France. The difference in the Phoenician images portrayed in the *Iliad* and in the *Odyssey* reflects this change faithfully. In the *Iliad* their wares are fit for gods and kings, while in the *Odyssey* they are a bunch of treacherous thieves. In the sixth century BC, conditions stabilized, with the Phoenicians controlling the coasts of Syria, North Africa and Spain, while the Greeks firmly established themselves in the Aegean and Black Seas, South Italy and southern France. Cyprus and Sicily continued to be a battle ground between the two, with Etruscan sea-power playing an enigmatic role on the Italian scene. In the fifth century, after the conclusion of the Persian wars, the Greeks penetrated the eastern Mediterranean in force, in preparation for the Hellenistic period, while the western Phoenicians were developing their Punic civilization, soon to clash with that of Rome.

An interesting aspect of the colonizing period is the gap which separates the dates mentioned in the historical sources for the foundation of the colonies, and the first archaeological evidence of their existence, which is usually hundreds of years later. This gap is not yet satisfactorily explained, and constitutes a major ground of contention between the two disciplines. Modern research has also shown that, contrary to the traditional view, neither commerce nor religion was among the motives of colonization. Commerce followed colonization, and not vice versa, and religion was at best a cohesive force in the process. Neither Phoenicians nor Greeks ever thought in terms of empire and mission. But their cultural achievements depended to a large degree on the colonies, which made possible a lively exchange of goods and ideas.

In those days, even more so than today, commerce was a major way of spreading culture, and overseas colonies served as a radiating nucleus in their new surroundings. The alphabet is said to be the greatest gift the Mediterranean world received from the Phoenicians. Its diffusion has been associated with the democratization of culture – it put written knowledge within reach of every man. This most highly developed system of writing appeared first in texts from the seventeenth century BC, its predecessors being pictographic, ideographic and phonetic. An act of abstraction and simplification, absent from all previous systems, created the alphabet. While each culture developed its own variation, they all – Greek or Latin, Hebrew or Arabic – derived from the same source. The alphabet was the most instrumental tool to create the basic conditions for direct communications among the different peoples settled around the Mediterranean. Commercial ties were intensified and ideas – religious and otherwise – spread more easily.

The Phoenicians were associated with another cultural feature, the Tophet, which seems to be in the utmost contrast to their advanced civilization. Child sacrifice to the Molek is mentioned in the Bible as having been practised by the Canaanites in Jerusalem, and strongly denounced thereafter. The Greeks and Romans also looked with disgust at this barbarous aspect of their foes' civilization. Modern historiography and archaeology have gone far in trying to explain away the awful evidence. Recent excavations revealed vast sacrificial sanctuaries in Carthage (Tunisia), Motya (Sicily), Sulcis (Sardinia) and other Punic sites. They include thousands of urns containing the cremated remains of infants, small children and animals, in several layers spanning about six centuries of continuous use. Now there is no doubt that child sacrifice was indeed practised by the Phoenicians and diffused by them all over the Mediterranean. The model created by anthropologists, of the development from human sacrifice to animal substitutes and symbolic sacrifices, no longer holds, and the accepted doctrine of progress in morals and culture is seriously challenged.

One of the most vexed problems in human history concerns the political, economic and social ties between a metropolis and its colonies. In ancient

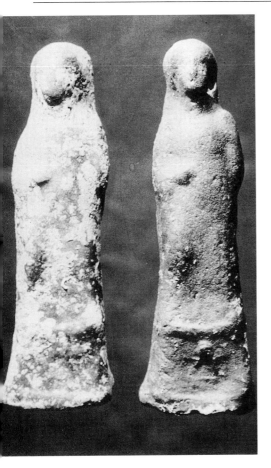

*The Phoenico–Punic chief goddess Tanit:* (left) *figurines of Shavey-Zion, Israel;* (right) *on a stele from Carthage with an inscription in the Punic alphabet*

times, the key to all these was religion and cult. From the sea of Shavey Zion, just south of the Phoenician metropolis Tyre, marine archaeologists retrieved hundreds of terracotta figurines, embodiments of the goddess Tanit, the Punic equivalent of Astarte. They throw interesting light on cult affiliations and cultural interrelations between the eastern and western basins of the Mediterranean. The goddess carries her own identity card, the symbol of Tanit in an abstract form, the dolphin and typical postures – her hands raised in benediction, she is pregnant or holding a child.

The Greek presence within Mediterranean civilization is so evident that it is often taken as its sole representative. Most conspicuous are the temples, always built to crown an outstanding natural background, very often a hill overlooking the sea. The Greek temple is not built inwards, it is directed outside and serves as a perfect casing for the god's statue within. Its standard of proportion and harmony could not be surpassed, although there were local variations. The Greek colonies east and west of the mother country, in Asia Minor and Sicily for instance, tried to build ever bigger, stronger and more impressive monuments, to express their independence and wealth, just as America has striven to outdo the Old World.

The Greek concept of the plastic arts became deeply rooted in all Mediterranean artistic creation, especially during the Hellenistic era. Its ideas of beauty, the handling of raw materials, the relationship between the abstract message and the natural features, the general and the particular – all gave a tremendous impetus to the development of art around the Mediterranean world. Cultures as alien to the Greek spirit as the Jewish in the East and the Iberian in the West incorporated the Greek artistic heritage into their most intimate culture, their burial grounds and fertility rites. After the conquests of Alexander the Great, the common culture of the Mediterranean reached a new peak. Another *oecumene*, this time dominated by Greek cultural values, arose in the eastern Mediterranean and radiated far to the West.

The fortunes of Greece depended on the sea, and the Greeks had a particular attitude towards it. In the heyday of Athenian power, Pericles is quoted as saying 'How then could men do anything worth mention who are tillers of the soil and not seamen?' (Thucydides, 1:142.7). But in 404, as a result of her defeat in the Peloponnesian War, Athens lost her empire and democracy was suppressed. Upon gaining control, Athens' new oligarchic rulers, the notorious thirty tyrants, made a symbolic move; they ordered that the Bema (a tribune from which speakers addressed the people), on the Pnyx hill, 'which had stood so as to look off towards the sea, to be turned so as to

*Artemis of Ephesus, the source of countless imitations all over the Mediterranean*

look inland, because they thought that maritime empire was the mother of democracy, and that oligarchy was less distasteful to tillers of the soil' (Plutarch, *Themistocles*, 19:4).

A famous Roman continued this line of thought (Cicero, *The Republic*, 2:10):

> Maritime cities also suffer a certain corruption and degeneration of morals, for they receive a mixture of strange languages and customs, and import foreign ways as well as foreign merchandise, so that none of their ancestral institutions can possibly remain unchanged. Even their inhabitants do not cling to their dwelling places, but are constantly tempted far from home by soaring hopes and dreams. . . . In fact, no other influence did more to bring about the final overthrow of Carthage and Corinth . . . due to the fact that the lust for trafficking and sailing seas had caused them to abandon agriculture and the pursuit of arms. Many things, too, that cause ruin to states as being the incitements to luxury are supplied by the sea, entering either by capture or import; and even the mere delightfulness of such a site brings in its train many an allurement to pleasure through either extravagance or indolence. And what I said of Corinth may perhaps be said with truth of the whole of Greece . . . for surrounded as [Greece and its islands] are by the billows, not only themselves but also the customs and institutions of their cities can be said to be afloat. . . . Clearly the cause of the evils and the revolutions to which Greece has been subject is to be traced to those disadvantages which I have just mentioned briefly as peculiar to maritime cities. But, nevertheless, with all these disadvantages they possess one great advantage – all the products of the world can be brought by water to the city in which you live, and your people in turn can convey or send whatever their own fields produce to any country they like.

Paradoxically, the final Greek conquest of the eastern Mediterranean basin was carried out by Alexander the Great strictly by land. Rome was the first to realize that the sea is not only a barrier but a bridge leading straight into enemy territory. Rome first used the sea to dispatch its armies everywhere, then as a convenient way to supply itself and the empire. The five hundred years of Roman domination revealed some characteristics of the Mediterranean region. The densely populated lands to the north, which enjoy abundant rainfall and fertile soil, natural resources and good ports, had the upper hand over the North African Punic coast, a mostly desert country, poor in human and natural resources, and over the East, divided upon itself and exhausted with trying to impose Greek culture on the local population.

Under Roman rule, Mediterranean culture reached a degree of uniformity unattained before or after. A traveller by sea would find himself, no matter where he landed, in Alexandria or Tyre, Nice or Tarragona, in a familiar atmosphere, which included all the amenities that were considered by the Romans as essential to civilized life. Roman language, Roman law and administration, Roman coins were adopted by all Mediterranean people, and constituted the bases for many future developments, such as the Romanesque languages, the medieval coinage systems, and the church administrative system. The similar way of life developed an international, cosmopolitan culture. For the first – and last – time in history, the Mediterranean was politically, as well as culturally, one world. For over two hundred years, the Pax Romana, peace under Roman rule, reigned over it. The volume of movement on sea and land was greater than ever before, as was its scope, which reached from India to the North Sea. The French scholar Jean Roujé and the American Lionel Casson have vastly deepened our knowledge of the maritime aspects of Greek and Roman civilization.

Around the Mediterranean, rich Romans and local VIPs had their villas by the sea, while people from all walks of life went on holiday to the beach resorts. In Italy, the most popular stretch of coast was the Bay of Naples, with Baiae as the most celebrated spot. Baiae subsided into the sea, and is now being explored; the finds there are astonishing. Many Roman villas have been excavated, others were depicted in murals; some are being recon-structed, to show the splendour of these homes and their owners' almost romantic involvement with the sea.

When the Mediterranean became an inner lake, the Empire's borders around it stretched for about 10,000 Roman miles (over 15,000 km). In comparison with the length of its borders, the Empire's population was too small to keep them effectively, since a good part of its area was occupied by empty marine space. The inner lake contributed to the well-being of the Empire, but weakened its resistance. When the Germanic people invaded the region in the third century AD, the borders collapsed, and in the fifth century the Byzantine Empire, or New Rome, ruled only the eastern parts.

It was the elaborate system of Roman rule around the Mediterranean that conditioned the spread of Christianity. The apostles travelled by sea and round the coasts, founding the first Christian communities along their routes. Later communications among these communities were also carried by sea, as was the Christianizing effort of the Byzantine emperors. The loss of Byzantine naval command and communications with North Africa was to a large extent the reason for the Islamization of these provinces, so deeply Christian in the preceding centuries. The Eastern Roman Empire was never fully resigned to this loss. The Byzantinologist H. Ahrweiler considers this infatuation with sea-power 'a cancer which sapped the Empire's strength' for centuries, contributing to its external and internal problems.

The Muslim conquest dealt a death blow to the prospects of reuniting the Mediterranean under Christian rule. Its most striking feature was its speed, which was followed by the thorough Islamization of the conquered populations. This was not done only by the sword; the new religion had a deep and widespread appeal. In the first half of the eighth century, a new *oecumene* seemed to be born; there was a Muslim presence from the gates of Constantinople to the heart of France. But Byzantine and Frankish resistance checked this expansion, and the Mediterranean was divided for over a thousand years, from the eighth to the eighteenth centuries, between Islam and Christianity.

The Muslim Empire brought the Mediterranean into direct contact with the influence of central Asiatic and even Far Eastern civilizations. In innumerable ways pertaining to the arts and sciences, as well as to everyday life, Islam enriched the cultural heritage of the classical world. The sciences of mathematics and physics, astronomy and medicine, religious and lay architecture, the manufacture of high-quality objects of metal, glass and of textiles, were all developed in the various centres of Islamic rule through the centuries, from Toledo and Seville to Mahdia and Palermo, Cairo and Alexandria, Damascus and Aleppo. During the 'Lesser Rennaissance' of the twelfth and thirteenth centuries, this golden cultural heritage was passed on to the West, through the contact areas in Spain and Sicily, as well as indirectly through other channels.

Thus the Mediterranean became the scene of the most fertile marriage of ideas, the combination of the Greek ideal of natural beauty with the tough moral code of the desert people, expressed in the monotheistic religions. Then came the efficiency and practicality of the Roman world, the instinctive vitality of the Germanic people and the sophisticated quietism of the Muslims. Other peoples – the Huns, the Slavs, the Turks and Black Africans – also contributed their share to the common heritage of the Mediterranean, but to a lesser degree. It seems that this unbelievable complexity finds its best expression in the Norman Kingdom of Sicily, and especially under its last ruler, Frederic II (Hohenstaufen), some of whose ideas on tolerance and coexistence could well be invoked today.

The location of Sicily at the heart of the Mediterranean Sea, where East meets West and North meets South, allows it to stand as an emblem of the whole, a palimpsest of cross-fertilization. A highlight of Sicilian history is the Norman Kingdom, which lasted for about two centuries (mid-eleventh to mid-thirteenth). It stood out in medieval Europe as a precocious experiment in cultural pluralism, with input from all preceding Mediterranean cultures, perfectly harmonized by the Norman genius of adaptability and practicality. This glorious culture radiated its influence as far as England, ruled at the time by another Norman house, and equally far to the Principality of Antioch, founded in the framework of the First Crusade.

The Norman Kingdom of Sicily was the first in Europe to revive the minting of gold coins, a turning point in a development which would lead Europe to the economic mastery of the world. Most of the modern monetary systems are based on the coinage which evolved in the Mediterranean basin from the seventh century BC, with many of the ancient names still in use – *drachma, shekel, dinar, lira*. Coinage, like the alphabet, constituted another big step towards turning the Mediterranean into one sea, facilitating transactions and affirming political and economic strength. Coins as such and in their capacity as medals are an important source for Mediterranean history. No wonder maritime themes and motifs play a dominant role in them. Numismatics, after the Byzantine coin *numisma*, is an important component in the study of economics and other fields of human activity.

The Norman Kingdom of Sicily was a child of the crusading movement, an exception to its generally militant and fanatical character. Although the main achievements of the crusades were the work of the feudal nobility, at times they constituted a true popular movement, fed by Messianic expectations. A generation after the conquest of the Holy Land, a French chronicler reported:

Consider, I pray, and reflect, how in our time God has transformed the Occident into the Orient. For we who were Occidentals have now become Orientals. He who was a Roman or a Frank has in this land been made into a Galilean or a Palestinean. He who was of Rheims or Chartres has now become a citizen of Tyre or Antioch. We have already forgotten the places of our birth; already these are unknown to many of us, or not mentioned any more. Some already possess homes or households by inheritance. Some have taken wives not only of their own people but Syrians or Armenians or even Saracens who have obtained the grace of Baptism. . . . Some tend vineyards, others till fields. People use the eloquence and idioms of diverse languages in conversing back and forth. Words of different languages have become common property known to each nationality. . . . He who was born a stranger is now as one born here; he who was born an alien has become a native. Our relatives and parents join us from time to time, sacrificing, even though reluctantly, all that they formerly possessed. Those who were poor in the Occident, God makes rich in this land. . . . God does not wish those to suffer want, who with their crosses dedicated themselves to follow Him, nay even to the end. You see therefore that this is a great miracle and one which the whole world ought to admire.

In reality, the crusaders were a two-hundred-year-long precarious European presence in the heart of the Muslim world, with hardly an attempt at communication or coexistence. Besides impressive monuments in the form of various fortifications, and many blue-eyed, blond-haired descendants, the crusaders did not leave a lasting impact in the East. The Holy Sepulchre fell again under Muslim rule; the Muslim counter-crusade revived the Gihad movement, and its success against the crusaders is a source of inspiration to this day. For the Europeans, the anticlimax caused by the failure of the movement and the criticism it aroused gave great impetus to missionary activities, so important in the modern colonial expansion of Europe. The crusading and missionary zeal is still alive, although sometimes uncons-ciously, in contemporary politics, especially in European attitudes to the Middle East.

From the Third Crusade on, most of the traffic to and from the Holy Land was carried by sea. This enhanced the importance of maritime transport and the position of the Italian powers, which handled most of it. Having conquered the Holy Land, the Mamluks devastated the coasts; they feared subsequent crusades, for maritime hegemony still rested with the West. In the wake of the crusades, minor European colonies remained in the Morea (the medieval Peloponnese), the Aegean islands and Cyprus, serving mainly as bases for the elaborate shipping system. From the thirteenth to the fifteenth centuries, the Mediterranean became an Italian lake, with Venetian and Genoese shipping lines carrying an intensive trade all over this sea and beyond. After a period of French cultural dominance, which coincided with the crusader movement, and was expressed by troubadours' songs of chivalrous values, Italian prosperity and leadership brought about the Renaissance of the classical world. Nevertheless, as the medieval economic historian R.S. Lopez, who coined the expression 'the commercial revolution',

*An eleventh-century business letter of the Cairo Geniza written in Arabic with Hebrew letters*

points out:

> So much has been said about the military and legal exploits of the
> Italians in the days of Rome and about their literary and artistic
> production during the Renaissance and after, that the man in the street
> is led to forget another gift of that gifted nation to the modern world –
> the creation, in the later Middle Ages, of the prototype of the modern
> commercial economy.

Alongside the mainstream of Mediterranean culture there constantly flowed
another current, both an exception and a model of the main one. The Jewish
people, who had lost their independence and been almost exterminated in
their home country in the first and second centuries AD, dispersed all around
the Mediterranean; the various communities kept close contact. In the dark
ages, the Jews played a major role in keeping communications and cultural
relations alive in the Mediterranean basin (see Chapter 6). These 'dark Middle
Ages' are darker because of our lack of information on them. Medieval
archaeology is not very attractive on the whole to Mediterranean scholars,
who are busy with the earlier strata of civilization; and upheavals which took
place during the fifth to the tenth centuries AD seem to have obliterated most
of the written documentation in every field except religious affairs. This
general darkness, especially in the social and economic aspects of life, is lit by
a unique source, the Cairo Geniza. This consists of a medley of many
thousands of documents, which were cast into the back room of a synagogue
in Old Cairo; because they bore the name of God, they could not be destroyed.
They portray the life of the Jewish community, mainly under Fatimid rule,
with its centres in Tunis and Cairo but with ties all over the Mediterranean
and Indian Ocean; all were deeply engaged in maritime trade. S.D. Goitein,
who has traced the Geniza documents in various collections from Cambridge
to Leningrad and studied them in depth, calls this community 'A
Mediterranean Society' *par excellence*.

In the late Middle Ages, when the economic need for the Jews was not as
urgent and the rising bourgeoisie took over most of their business, their
persecution began in most European countries. The crusading movement,
and especially the Spanish reconquest, added a strong religious motive; this
persecution culminated in the expulsion of the Jews from Spain and other
countries. In the sixteenth century the uprooted Jewish communities moved
north and east and became the economic mainstay of the newly founded
Ottoman Empire. Typical was Don Joseph Nassi and his mother-in-law Dona

Grazia, very influential figures in the Sultan's court in the 1560s, who dreamed of bringing their people back to Zion to welcome the awaited Messiah.

The Ottoman rise to power in the eastern Mediterranean balanced the achievement of the Christian powers in the West, which was crowned by the unification of Spain and the fall of Granada in 1492. About fifty years earlier, in 1453, the Ottomans took Constantinople, the millennial capital of the Byzantine Empire. From there they threatened communications in the whole Mediterranean by conquering Rhodes, Cyprus and the Morea, and besieging Malta, while their young offensive navy also took North Africa. Although checked at Lepanto in 1572, the Ottomans strained the traditional Mediterranean commercial system, while great oceanic discoveries and the rise of the national states in Western Europe made for a loss of interest in the Middle Sea. The capital cities developed inland, in regions more central to the new states and farther from danger, and the coastal areas decayed.

The Slavs reached the Mediterranean at about the same time as the Muslims, and they have been there ever since. It is true that their mark was not felt as much as that of the Arabs and Turks, but they were the originators of the word 'slave' (*sclavus*), a sinister part of Mediterranean civilization that was later exported all over the world. The people of Yugoslavia and other parts of the Balkan peninsula had always struggled, not only against the Turks but against difficult natural conditions, and had become expert seafarers and redoubtable pirates. Dubrovnik is one of the Mediterranean's best preserved medieval port towns, with a charm comparable to that of Venice. In the villages and cities of the Dalmatian coast, the Muslim call for prayer hovers over Catholic churches full of very orthodox icons and incense. It is in the Balkans that the Mediterranean cultural stew is probably the thickest and most flavourful.

Napoleon's campaign to the east in 1799 was a new turning point in Mediterranean history. The north-west again felt strong and rich enough to start an offensive. The campaign failed, but the naval superiority of the European powers over 'the sick man of the Bosporus' was clearly manifested. The French conquest of Algeria in 1830 was the first step in the seizure of North Africa and the Levant by the European powers. This was completed by the end of the First World War, when the Turkish Empire disintegrated completely. The French took Tunis (1881), Morocco (1912) and Syria (1920); the Italians took Libya (1912), and the British, Cyprus (1878), Egypt (1882) and Palestine (1918). Imperialism and colonialism are bad words in today's political vocabulary, but this was in many ways an essential phase in the

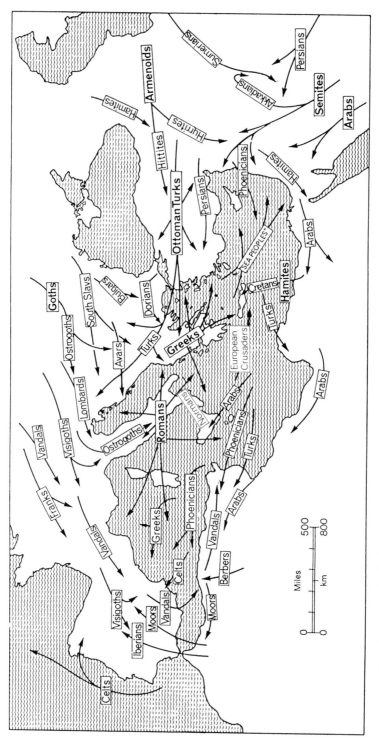

*Migration waves in the Mediterranean region*

history of the less developed peoples, which enabled them to enter the twentieth century and establish new states on the ruins of old empires. Between the two world wars the Mediterranean was once more an *oecumene*, ruled by the European powers and constituting again, thanks to the Suez Canal, a link in the international communications chain. The Second World War broke up this unity, re-dividing the sea between the allied and the axis countries.

During the nineteenth and twentieth centuries, most Mediterranean countries gained their independence,. usually after fierce and protracted battles. This solved some problems, but others have emerged. There are still some residues of the past, like the British presence in Gibraltar. Malta, another British stronghold, has gained its independence, and is emerging as an active centre of Mediterranean co-operation, as befits its geographical location.

In this process, conditions in some places deteriorated to the point where, from the middle of the nineteenth century, emigration became the dominant fact in the life of Mediterranean people. Many millions left Syria and Lebanon, Greece and Italy, Spain and Portugal, to find a better life in the New World, mainly in North and South America. Lebanese literature in the Argentine has surpassed that of the harassed homeland, while the Sicilian Mafia in the US is far more dangerous than its original. Many others make a seasonal or temporary migration from the developing countries to the industrial centres in the north. Are Mediterranean countries losing their youth, their wealth, their individuality? Is the process at all reversible?

Several times in its history the Mediterranean was a whole. In the middle of the second millennium BC, during the ElAmarna Age, the eastern basin was one; Mesopotamian, Egyptian, Canaanite and Greek myths and traditions cross-fertilized each other, resulting in the Greek and Hebrew classics, of which Homer and the Bible are the greatest. There followed a period of hiatus and constant warring between Phoenicians and Greeks, Punics and Romans. The Hellenistic world created a new *oecumene*, still mainly in the eastern basin, but stretching far into the Middle East and the West. Then came the apex – the Roman Empire, which was more of a common civilization than a cultural superstructure. The cultural unity came with Christianity, but by that time political and economic cohesion was long lost. With the advent of Islam, the Mediterranean was torn in two or three; new factors came on to the scene all through the Middle Ages. This division has lasted the longest; it is still in existence.

The Mediterranean, this old cradle of civilization, drained of its life blood by political, economic and social strains, is now engulfed in a whirlpool of conflicting currents. On the one hand, western material culture has permeated every part of personal and public life. On the other hand, and largely as a reaction to the above process, religious and national fundamentalism are increasingly gaining ground. A third current pulls in the direction of a wider orbit – the EEC, African Unity, the Arab League and the like. The Mediterranean world of the past has known how to assimilate different cultural influences and fuse them into a balanced, pluralistic whole, though it has so often been divided and torn apart by power play struggles along its shores. Will it be able to revive itself and define its new identity? In this fight for Mediterranean cultural survival, there is hope for other parts of our world. The tides of history may yet create a new Mediterranean *oecumene*, with a firm economic and political basis, but going beyond them to include the spirit and positive values of the common Mediterranean cultural heritage, which still has so much to offer the world at large at the dawn of a new millennium.

CHAPTER 12

# THE CALL OF THE SEA

O N  T H E  T H R E S H O L D  of the twenty-first century we are entering the
third phase of our relationship with the sea. In the beginning there was
fear, a primordial awe of this vast and unpredictable element. Then came
several thousand years of struggle, during which man has learnt to live by the
sea and love it. Today, although we still have these feelings, we are entering a
new phase, the most intimate in the history of man and sea. It is

> the age of Aquarius. A time of splendid adventure. A time when man
> stepped off the earth – into space and into the sea. . . . There are
> intriguing parallels between spaceman and underwater-man. Both
> dwell in extra-earth environments. One environment is an ethereal
> vacuum of no pressures, while the other is a dense liquid of high
> pressures. . . . The footprints of man leading into the sea are excitingly
> similar to those forged into space.

Diving, that direct contact with the sea, is within reach of everybody,
opening a further dimension of the old man-and-sea relationship. The new
intimacy breeds a new kind of myth, the modern tales of divers and
submarine crews. When divers talk of their experiences, they seem to go
back to the remote origins of the species, to treat the sea as the ancestral
mother; immersion in it resembles our original immersion in amniotic fluid.
Silent, three-dimensional slow motion movement invigorates, the sea acts as a
source of energy. But sometimes, also, they talk of accidents.

The untamed sea is still a threat, even at our relatively advanced stage of
knowledge and technology. In the past, man stood helpless before the giant
sea, which seemed eager to engulf everything, including earth itself. He
looked for benign intercessors with the destructive forces of nature; and one
of the earliest such partners was the dolphin, a friendly and playful creature
very common in all parts of the Mediterranean. It is a central motif in

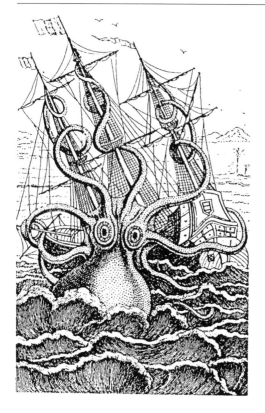

*Left: Sea monsters in the* Histoire Naturelle *by Buffon*

*Right: The temple of Aphrodite in Cyprus on a local coin and a reconstruction*

Mediterranean cultures, reaching as far as the Nabateans, a desert people who roamed the Levant in Roman times. The dolphin is depicted in countless forms, on coins, mosaics and statues, usually in a variation on the themes of a boy rescued by a dolphin, the dolphin helping fishermen with their nets, or the dolphin as the symbol of the gods – Poseidon, Apollo, Tanit.

Ancient literary sources reveal a long tradition of the duty to propitiate the sea. An Egyptian papyrus credits Astarte as the one who revokes the tribute to the sea, which the Egyptian gods were obliged to pay. This was a recurrent theme of Middle Eastern mythology; the story of Jonah has its origins in a sacrifice to an angry sea-god. While the eastern myths are known to us only in fragmentary form, a full and complex Greek sea mythology reached us. For the coastal Greeks, the sea must have been all-pervasive; Poseidon with his bursts of bad temper dominated their lives just as his temple still dominates the sea at cape Sounion. Their sea was alive with sea-nymphs, the *nereids*, Poseidon's daughters with silvery feet and golden hair, who competed with the dolphins for fun in the calm sea; with *tritons*, sea-satyrs in the form of young men with fish tails, blowing conches through the storms. Aphrodite the 'foamborn', the goddess of desire, was as central to them as Astarte her predecessor was to the Phoenicians, and as Venus was later to the Romans. Countless statues attest to this fact, some of them found appropriately in the sea.

These pagan beliefs and rites are strongly alive today, although clad in Christian, Muslim and Jewish names and symbols. Along the Ionian coast of

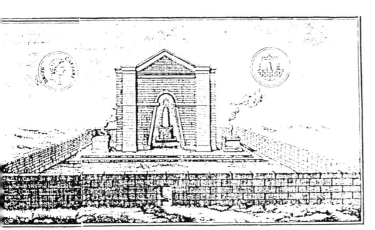

Sicily, a strange festival takes place each year on 24 June, San Giovanni's day. Many fishing boats go out to sea with their crew; suddenly there is a cry of 'a fish in the water' and all the fishermen try to catch it. The fish is in fact the best swimmer amongst the young men, and for the occasion he is called Cola (or Nicola). He is caught, escapes, and caught again, this time wounded, with the red blood colouring the sea around him. This must be a relic of an ancient rite, simulating the desired turn of events for the important hunt of the swordfish. The Sirenes, already present in the *Odyssey*, appear regularly in North African popular mythology. Every stray whale, dolphin or large fish revives popular interest in sea monsters, a common theme in seamen's stories through the ages. On their high holidays, religious Jews go to the seashore and empty their pockets in a symbolic act of purification – Tashlich – following Micah (7:19), 'Thou wilt cast all their sins into the depths of the sea'. This ritual of purification by the sea goes back to the *Iliad* (1:312–317), and probably even further, deep into prehistoric times.

Before lighthouses were built, most ports were marked by an elevated area, topped by a statue or a temple, dedicated first to Astarte and Poseidon, then later to Mary, Aghios Elias or St Nicholas. Churches like the Santa Maria Stella Maris and Notre Dame de la Garde occupy the very locations of the old temples of Astarte, Aphrodite and Venus. Some local traditions embody these cultural transformations. In north-western Sicily, Eryx (Erice) was the centre of a widespread pagan cult of the fertility goddess, protectress of the seafarers. This cult was suppressed by the church, but continued its secret life underground, and re-emerged after more than a thousand years. In 1570, a boat carrying a painting of the Madonna and Child was miraculously saved from a terrible storm just below Erice. A church was built for the painting in the village of Custonaci nearby, and every year in August, a procession used to carry the painting uphill to Erice and down again. Now the people of Custonaci have stopped this procession, and replaced it with another, going down to the sea. The Neapolitan Santa Lucia, the Madonna della Catena (the chain closing the harbour, see Chapter 5), gave her name to an internationally popular song, and also to the little suburb by the port, where Pizza Napolitana may have been born, and where, on the last Sunday in August, the ancient sea festival of the 'Nzegna is celebrated.

Stes-Maries-de-la-Mer is a fortress church visible for miles across land and sea, at the heart of the Camargue, the marshy Rhône delta. According to Provençal legend, not long after the crucifixion of Jesus Christ, a dark-skinned servant, Sara, her mistress St Mary Salome (mother of the apostles James and John), St Mary Jacobe and some say also Mary Magdalene and Martha, fled the Holy Land. Though their boat had neither sail nor oar, they crossed the Mediterranean and finally put ashore at this desolate spot. Tradition has it that Sara was the first to sow the seeds of Christianity among the local gypsy tribes. She has never been canonized in Rome, but on her saint's day, 24 May, gypsies by the thousand flock from far and wide to venerate their patron saint, and take the statue of her and those of her companions back into the water so that they can give the sea their blessing. A great festival follows, with bullfights and races with the famous Camargue horses.

In Ephesos, an ancient Greek town in today's Turkey, the most venerated goddess, Artemis, was worshipped by the whole Greek world. Imitations of her Ephesian attire are found from Spain to Egypt. In the early Middle Ages, not long after the establishment of Christianity, another revered site was erected nearby – the church of St Mary. Also in the eastern Mediterranean, in Cyprus, where the original Aphrodite was said to have been born near

*Poseidon rides again: crossing the causeway to Motya, Sicily*

Paphos, a peculiar development has taken place; her temple in Kouklia contained no image, but an abstract form, for she was too beautiful to be visualized. As described and depicted on coins, the statue was in the shape of a large, shiny black conical stone, which was found near the temple. Tanit, her Punic counterpart who was all-dominant in Carthage and her colonies, was also usually rendered by an abstract symbolic sign. In the north-west corner of Cyprus, about 25 km from Paphos, a natural beauty spot is called 'the baths of Aphrodite' or *Fontana Amorosa*, and was very popular in the Middle Ages as it is to this day.

The most amazing of all later shrines in Cyprus is a Muslim version in Hala Sultan Tekke, near Larnaca. This pretty mosque and *zawiya* are dedicated to Umm Haram, who was an aunt of the Prophet, and her namesake, the wife of one of the Muslim conquerers of Cyprus, who followed him and was killed on that spot. This holy place ranks after Mecca, Medina and Jerusalem as a Muslim place of pilgrimage, and was greatly venerated in Ottoman times. Every Turkish ship passing by used to dip its flag in its honour. A holy place dedicated to a woman is quite rare in Islam, and relates to the strong Aphrodite tradition.

The followers of Christ, Peter and Paul, were connected with the sea as fishermen and missionary travellers. They were amalgamated into the mainstream of Mediterranean tradition by their identification with the Dioscuri, the brothers Castor and Pollux of Greek and Roman mythology, who turned into the constellation Gemini; as such they help mariners in their navigation and offer miraculous deliverance in desperate situations. They appear as two faint lights on both sides of the mast, signalling deliverance, or by their signs – the helmet and the star (as on the ram of Athlit, see Chapter 10). Thus they are depicted in the church of Cefalu, Sicily. St Nicholas is another guardian saint of mariners and fishermen (as well as thieves and children). The vicissitudes of his transformation from a martyred bishop to Santa Claus are a fascinating theme to follow.

The votive offerings presented at these shrines and the traditional prayers that go with them have a fundamental and universal quality, and can be adapted to any religious framework. Thus this Maltese prayer:

> O Lady of Ta Pinu
> Let me not perish!
> For the sake of
> The love you bore
> Your divine Son –
> Rescue me!

A Venetian version of the church hymn goes:

> Keep safe from stormy weather, Oh Lord,
> All your faithful mariners,
> Safe from sudden shipwreck and from evil
> Unsuspected tricks of cunning enemies.

Since the *Odyssey*, the sea journey and its circumstances have transcended the material, realistic dimension. It collected mythological and psychological overtones and became the symbol of struggle, of the greatest human journey of all, life itself. Obversely, the sea can also stand for escape and death, sleep and oblivion, while the arrival safely on shore, the great return – *nostos* – is the comeback of the intelligent mind, of memory and enlightened life. When saints came into the picture, they served as guiding angels, rewarding faith and hope with final deliverance. Later the compass became the symbol of the right course to follow. Today, scientists conduct experiments not only into the technical aspects of ancient seafaring; they also try to relive the old myths

*Odysseus and the Sirens depicted on an Attic vase, fifth century BC (above)*

*Odysseus pursued by The North Wind, Boreas, on a satirical vase*

and gain a deeper understanding of the psychological factors at play.

Robert Foulke, a professor of literature, has actually sailed in the wake of Odysseus, claiming that from the *Odyssey*,

> in works ranging from the voyages collected by Hakluyt in the last decades of the sixteenth century through stories written by Conrad at the beginning of the twentieth, there is usually no clear demarcation between fact and fiction, experience and imagination. Among all narrative forms, the voyage pattern clings to the inescapable realities of life at sea, on the one hand, and simultaneously projects human desires and fantasies, on the other . . . seafarers find their sense of space suggesting infinity and solitude . . . and prison-like confinement. The seafarers' sense of time is equally complex; it is both linear and cyclical, linear in the sense that voyages have beginnings and endings, departures and landfalls . . . yet time is also cyclical, just as the rhythm of waves is cyclical, because the pattern of the ship's daily routine, watch on and watch off, highlights endless recurrence. . . . Voyages out are a natural mode for the human imagination exploring the unknown, whether it be discovering new continents, finding out the truth about the self, or reaching worlds more perfect or flawed than this one.

The myths of the journey and the return took on a different meaning in the framework of the religious pilgrimage (see Chapter 8). In the secular modern world, the pilgrimage has been replaced by the cultural tour. In the eighteenth century, the *grand tour* of the Mediterranean became a must in aristocratic and artistic circles. In the nineteenth century, the Mediterranean was a major source of artistic inspiration in every creative field, from painting and poetry to music and architecture. At the end of the twentieth century, art has become international and one can hardly define any cultural creativity beyond the traditional ethnic level as local or national. Nevertheless, there is a definite set of associations with terms like Mediterranean music and Mediterranean architecture. Is this another myth, or is there a Mediterranean quality at the basis of the fertile and varied creation of Mediterranean people?

*'Peindre dans la lumière de la Méditerranée'* became almost an obsession, especially with the French. They extol its luminosity, the transparent air, the white-washed houses against the background of the sea, and the colourful sunsets. Mediterranean light is too fierce for gentle colour variations. It made northern painters discover the sharp contrast of light and shade. It also made

them use strong colours that were not to be seen before – lemon-yellow, Prussian blue, and the purple-violet of the shadows. Van Gogh memorably captured Mediterranean light, and so did Gauguin, who went even further to the Pacific islands, but was basically a Mediterranean artist *par excellence*. Matisse painted mostly interiors, getting much of his inspiration in North Africa. Picasso who grew up by the Mediterranean had a different source of inspiration; not Mediterranean colours, but the pristine cultural heritage of the Mediterranean spirit. This was best expressed in his work in Antibes – the minotaur, bullfights, bathing women, the ceramic art. A special museum in Antibes, on the French Riviera, exhibits this phase of his work; against the background of the sea, there is an exhilarating and purifying quality to these works, composed mostly in smiling colours and full of *joie de vivre*. With today's Mediterranean painters the sea moves from the background to the front; it is now the topic of the picture itself, an abstract and concrete presence at one and the same time.

Popular Mediterranean music is very much alive today, in spite of the heavy input of international rhythm. Greek and Turkish, Egyptian and Moroccan, Spanish and Italian songs and instrumental pieces are constantly transmitted by the media, and not only in their countries of origin. It would appear that some kind of Pan-Mediterranean music is being born, a fresh mixture made up of the traditional trends. This happened in the past at periods of strong intercultural fertilization, in a process similar to that of the spoken language (see Chapters 8 and 11). Most Mediterranean music is clearly non-western; it is based on rhythms with irregular divisions and asymmetrical metre; its melodies based on sensuous, florid improvisation, with intervals smaller than the semitone; the human voice plays a primary role, with an unclear boundary between song and speech; intricate melody and complex rhythm do not have to accommodate each other, and this music has a multidimensional quality. In the music of the concert hall, there is also a category which may be called Mediterranean, although this kind of music is certainly part and parcel of the whole range of continental influences. This is especially true of the opera – the clarity and lightness of Saint-Saëns, the romanticism of Verdi, the melodrama of Puccini. There are composers and musicologists, like Charles Camilleri of Malta, who believe that 'Mediterranean music shows there are possibilities of transcending the Western-non-Western dichotomy, opportunities for the various traditions of mankind to converge and interpenetrate each other, in a richer and more comprehensive language. . . .'

In some fields, the Mediterranean spirit had to go as far as America and come back, in order to break through the resistance of conservative tradition. Isadora Duncan, the real initiator of modern dance, drew her inspiration from ancient Greece and opened the way for a long line of innovators, who rediscovered natural movement and elevated ethnic origins to the stage. In architecture also, the Mediterranean style penetrated its original ground only after having been pioneered elsewhere; the inner-space (patio) and flat roof, the stout curved exterior lines with few openings, the clustered beehive habitation. Since many Mediterranean countries are developing rapidly, these basic features are endlessly repeated in housing and tourist dwellings, with a strong tendency to exaggeration and artificiality, as in the *pueblo español* style condominiums, the totally identical 'Greek island' villages, and the ubiquitous 'oriental arches'. The genius of the Catalan Gaudi, the Italian Nervi, Moshe Safdie, who created the 'habitat' for Expo 67 in Montreal, Canada, and institutes such as the Centre d'Architecture de la Mer (CAM) in southern France, balance these outrages and point to more discretion in the use of Mediterranean motifs in the future.

Goethe and Flaubert, Byron and Graves are a few of a long line of writers and poets for whom the Mediterranean was a focal point of inspiration, a reservoir of the spirit rather than a place name. As with northern painters, the Mediterranean presence for northern writers was light and warmth, rustic simplicity on the one hand, and great cultural heritage on the other, the romance of the East and the exoticism of the South. Above all, the Mediterranean became known to the world through travel memoirs, which by definition are an outsider's view. The works of Lawrence and Gerald Durrell (though not travellers, they are not natives either) did more to enhance the general awareness of Mediterranean atmosphere in the middle of our century than any native literature. Through them, a new literary *genre* was born which the French call *le génie du lieu* (the spirit of place).

While European countries like Spain and France, Italy and Greece, have produced writers of international fame – Jimenez, Camus, Pirandello and Seferis (all Nobel prize winners) – the rest of Mediterranean literature is much less well known. But it is in the process of asserting itself; it holds great promise in store.

A Mirror for Beirut 1967

The street is a woman who says
The *fatiha* when she's grieved
Or make the sign of the Cross.

Under her breast
The hunchbacked night
Fills his bag
With his grey whining dogs
And snuffed out stars.

The street is a woman who bites
The passerby.
The camel sleeping around her breast
Sings
For the oil shaikhs.
And the street is a woman who falls
On her bed.

Adunis (Syro-Lebanese)


The End of Elul

I'm tired of summer.
The smoke rising from the convent of the silent nuns
Is all I have to say.
This year winter will come late
When we're ready for its coming,
And we won't be.

I'm tired. And curse the three Great Religions,
Which won't let me sleep at night
What with bells and howls of muezzins and loud *shofars*
    and noisy atonements.
Oh, God, close your houses, let the world rest.
Why hast thou *not* forsaken me?
This year the year hesitates.
The summer drags on.
If it weren't for the tears that I have kept back all these years.
I'd have dried up like thorns. . .

Y. Amichai (Israeli)

The role of the Mediterranean as a source of creative inspiration, especially in the arts, is now institutionalized in a long series of events, such as the Venetian plastic arts Biennale, the Cannes Film Festival, the multi-media meeting of the two worlds in Spoleto (*Festivale dei Due Mondi*), the Erice Music Festival, the comprehensive Naples Biennale Internazionale del Mare, and theatrical happenings in countless ancient and modern sites. They are meetings of the old world and the new, in time and in space, around the sea which is the mirror of Europe, Asia and Africa, and which reflects other stimuli from all parts of the world.

Venice, where the Biennale is held, is the place where the bond with the sea reached perhaps its greatest height. The Venetian medieval custom of the *sposalizio* symbolized Venice's inseparable link with the sea, and Venetian domination of the waters. The tradition is said to date back to 1177; it began with a famous pact between Pope and Emperor, and ceased only with the fall of the *Serenissima*, at the end of the eighteenth century. On Ascension Day, the Doge was rowed out in the *bucentoro*, a galley especially designed and gilded for stately occasions. With the leading men of the Republic and envoys of foreign states looking on, he cast a golden ring into the sea, saying 'By this ring I take dominion over you, as that of a husband over his wife.' This tradition is certainly an adaptation of an ancient pagan offering to Neptune, Poseidon or an even earlier sea god. In the Greek islands, a similar event takes place; a gold ring is thrown into the sea and the children compete in diving for it.

Venice today is a sad sight, a crumbling city often flooded by high water and tourist masses. Its palaces and art treasures, churches and piazzettas, alleys rich with exquisite workmanship, have recently been in real danger of inundation by the sea. Since the beginning of the century, a subsidence of 23 cm has been measured. The reasons for the sinking of Venice are complex, and necessitated a multidisciplinary plan of prolonged and costly research. Neither the city nor the Italian government would tackle the project alone and the future of Venice seemed doomed. After the floods of 1969, international concern co-ordinated by UNESCO brought about a collaborative effort, which had far-reaching results. It was discovered that overpumping of ground-water by the industries at Marghera, on the mainland opposite Venice and the lagoons, was a major cause of subsidence. Alternative solutions were developed and this was checked. However, occasional floods – *acqua alta* – continue to be a grave problem. Now the municipality, together with the big industries, have made a very large investment in the construction of dams designed to close up the 'mouths' of the lagoons when seas increase in the northern Adriatic. Although progress is slow and uneven, and the results are not yet fully visible, the attempt to save Venice stands out as a great triumph of conscientious humanity, Mediterranean solidarity and enlightened government.

Fear and love, aversion and fascination, fateful bond and eternal struggle, are at the base of man's relations with the sea. The role of the sea in the mind of modern man and its place in the field of recreation cannot be explained otherwise. But if our basic feelings are the same, other things have changed. For thousands of years, man has been involved with the sea and has had an effect on it. The sea has taxed man's ingenuity to the utmost; he has created better fishing methods and exploitation of marine resources, more manoeuvrable ships, efficiency in the harbours, economy in transportation, better navigational instruments, a safer and more comfortable life on board, better organization and security at sea, a greater command of the waters. But in the last century, human pressure on the sea and its immediate coasts has become so intense that it threatens to tip the balance and create a new kind of chaos.

The marine ecological problems in the world as a whole, and in the Mediterranean especially, are calling for a new common effort, to save the sea from the doom which could be caused by pollution, over-exploitation and conflicting demands. Our response should be in the vein of Nietzsche's *fröhliche Wissenschaft*; joyous science, informed instinct, the realization of the unity of life and knowledge, all of which are related to the Mediterranean spirit. Thus ecological problems which are specifically marine would serve as a basis for wider co-operation.

The lists of international conventions and regional agreements on ecological matters may be impressive, but the reality is that they are hardly effective as yet. Action has to come from the grass roots, and from the countries concerned, whose people should understand the situation best. It is not by mere chance that the smallest countries in the Mediterranean region, like Malta and Israel, are voicing their ideas most vehemently, each one for its own reasons. They are the first to realize the need for coexistence and co-operation. The larger countries around the Mediterranean may not feel the urgent need yet, but the times are calling for Pan-Mediterranean unity.

The main obstacle seems to be the implosive character of the area. The ecological and technical problems may be overcome, but the deeper cultural conflicts are harder to solve. It is high time for a constructive break with the old constants of war and division, if we are to create a new Mediterranean *oecumene*.

The countries bordering the Mediterranean are a political kaleidoscope; there are many areas of tension, a danger to the peace of the world at large. Economically, they represent conflicting interests. Culturally, the divergent historical development of these countries is a significant element of the mutual distrust in the region. Nevertheless, they share a common way of life around the sea, a common maritime civilization. It is these very differences – political, economic and cultural – which hold a great promise for the future. Co-operation among them would be an important step forward. UNESCO has already started a constructive initiative in this field by convening in Cordoba the representatives of the three Mediterranean historical religions – Christianity, Islam and Judaism. The Papacy is also more open to the possibilities of building bridges across the divide in this age of growing religious fundamentalism.

The Mediterranean, by its physical nature, can serve as the moderating agent among its surrounding countries. Culturally it has been, many times in the past, a true bridge for the interchange of materials and ideas. Narrow-minded fanaticism comes usually from inland, from the mountains and the deserts. Any progress achieved around this sea, any step towards reconciliation, collaboration and the peaceful solution of common problems, will certainly affect the whole world; the Mediterranean region is germane to the dialogue between Europe and the Third World, to the relations between East and West, as well as to the gap between the northern and southern hemispheres. The call of the sea is for tolerance and insight, respect for the past and hope for the future.

APPENDIX A

# MEDITERRANEAN ACTION PLAN (MAP)

Initiated at the Barcelona convention of 1975, under the auspices of UNEP, this project started by dividing the Mediterranean into thirteen regions, which corresponded to the inner seas and to other coastal and maritime areas. Immediate priority was given to making a sound assessment of the state of the Mediterranean and identifying its major problems. The Mediterranean Pollution Monitoring and Research Programme, or MedPol, was set up in phases to collect standardized compatible data from all concerned regarding general pollution – what is dumped and where, how much and how often.

Among other things, it has been found that about eighty-five per cent of the sewage flow into the sea is inadequately treated. Poisonous effluents from factories (mainly heavy metals) and from oil refineries are pumped into the sea, killing marine life and endangering human health by moving up the food chain (as in the case of mercury). Rivers carry pollutants of every type from far inland into the sea, at a rate that far exceeds that of direct discharge from coastal sources of pollution.

Up to a quarter of the waste oil discharged into the world seas by tankers and passenger liners, freighters and naval vessels, ends up in the Mediterranean, which is a cul-de-sac in the centre of the system. Thousands of tons of pesticides are transported by winds and washed with the rain into the sea, as well as enormous amounts of detergents and even radioactive materials. Many coastal lagoons and inlets are becoming uninhabitable. On the basis of data gathered in Phase I of MedPol, a long-term programme was set up. Phase II, for 1981–1990, continues the monitoring and research activities on a routine basis.

Other UN agencies, such as the Food and Agriculture Organization (FAO), the World Health Organization (WHO), the World Meteorological Organization (WMO), the Intergovernmental Oceanographic Commission (IOC) and the UN Educational, Scientific and Cultural Organization (UNESCO), are giving their full co-operation.

Several protocols were signed by all the countries concerned, giving the legal convention its practical force, and topics of special concern were noted:

1. The first protocol deals with the dumping of pollutants from ships and aircraft. It completely prohibits the dumping of the most dangerous wastes, which are on its 'black list', and seriously limits the dumping of less perilous materials, by a system of permits authorized only by UNEP itself. The first two vital questions to be tackled have been bathing beaches and mercury in seafood.

2. The second protocol commits the governments to co-operate in cases of emergencies at sea, which consist mainly of oil and other chemical spills. The oil-combating centre in Malta makes contingency plans on all levels, provides training in oil-pollution control, and helps to co-ordinate action in case of accidents.

3. The protocol on land-based sources of pollution has been adopted by a surprisingly large number of states, considering the high costs which are involved in its implementation. States, cities and industries have agreed to make the investments necessary to prevent pollution by sewage, industrial waste and the like. This protocol, like the one on dumping, has a black and a grey list. The total cost of its implementation is estimated at up to fifteen billion dollars within the next ten to fifteen years.

4. A special programme for protected areas and marine parks has its centre in Tunisia. More than a hundred sites were selected as having a particular standing in relation to certain species of plant and animal life unique to the Mediterranean, as well as to man and his cultural heritage. Unexpectedly, this programme is running into difficulties, with strong local opposition from such sectors as industry, tourism and the military.

5. The centre for the integrated planning of the development and management of the resources of the Mediterranean basin has its seat in Sofia-Antipolis in France. Here projections are made into the future, in the framework of the Blue Plan, which envisages alternative policies towards the years 2000 and 2025.

6. The more direct and practical side of these projections is organized by the centre in Split, Yugoslavia, which has a Priority Actions Programme dealing with such topics as the development of aquaculture, the rehabilitation of historic centres, the special case of islands and isolated coastal areas, earthquake zones, energy sources, and many other topics of general interest to all Mediterranean countries.

7. A new programme for the Rational Offshore Operation has recently been developed to regulate the risks of marine pollution deriving from the exploitation and exploration of the sea-bed and submarine soil.

8. A central unit has been set up in Athens, serving as the headquarters of MAP, co-ordinating its actions with the other international organizations, with the national governments and with the centres in Malta, Sofia-Antipolis, Split and Tunis. After a few initial years of heavy financial support from UNEP, MAP is now virtually self-sufficient and independent, maintained by the contributions of the Mediterranean governments concerned.

# UNDERWATER ARCHAEOLOGY

Since about 1900, hard-hat and free-divers (mostly sponge fishermen) have been lifting artifacts from the sea-bed. Some of the best pieces of Greek and Roman sculpture were discovered in this way. Since 1943, scuba divers have joined in, and amateurs enthusiastically explored the riches lying on the bottom. Jacques Cousteau, one of the pioneers of the new equipment, was the first to grasp the importance of a systematic approach. At that stage, the best that could be arranged was an underwater excavation supervised by an archaeologist sitting in a boat above the site; a dig of this nature was carried out in Grand Congloué, near Marseille, in 1952. Only in 1960 did Peter Throckmorton, an American archaeologist and diver, conduct the first project in which the archaeologists themselves did the diving, off Cape Gelidonya in Turkey.

All the first underwater excavations of ancient shipwrecks took place in the Mediterranean, particularly off the coasts of France and Italy: Albenga and Spargi, Grand Congloué and Titan. Here some of the basic techniques and instruments were developed and perfected. By trial and error, a new discipline evolved, from simple treasure-hunting underwater, to an exercise involving the same degree of accuracy as the most modern dig on land.

In spite of heavy limitations imposed by changing sea conditions, the length of the individual stay underwater (see Appendix D) and the use of essential instruments, the stratigraphy of the site and finds is followed meticulously by measuring on a three-dimensional grid the relative location of every find, and every minute detail is recorded. Because of these limitations and the much longer and more expensive process of excavation, the underwater dig, compared to its dry counterpart, usually devotes more time to preliminary surveys and preparations, and relies more heavily on technical aids such as detecting and sensoring devices, from the simple metal detector to the side-scanning and mud-penetrating sonar systems, photogrammetry, television and mini-submarines. This new discipline is now applied to every kind of underwater research as a matter of course, and is constantly incorporating new methods and tools developed in other fields of work underwater.

The American group which excavated at Cape Gelidonya and Kyrenia is now part of the Institute of Nautical Archaeology at Texas A & M University, which has founded a Mediterranean centre in Bodrum, Turkey. Its work has gained fame both for pioneering efforts and for scientific achievements. Among other finds, the remains of vessels from the fourteenth century BC to the eleventh century AD, with items of their respective cargoes, are on display in the castle of the Knights of St John in Bodrum, on the site of ancient Halicarnassos.

However great the progress, more than 90 per cent of the initial information concerning sunken ships and scattered cargo in the Mediterranean still comes from fishermen and sport divers. This is true of the small percentage of finds that are finally reported: most of them are presumably dug and sold illegally, as the authorities are powerless to check this. All Mediterranean countries are very concerned with this problem, some of them to the point of forbidding almost all kinds of diving along their shores, like Greece, which still suffers from the trauma of the looting of its treasures in the last century, and the fatal accidents which happened on the first archaeological digs. France may serve as an example of the opposite attitude. Its law concerning underwater activity is quite liberal, resulting in the intensive involvement of many divers, amateur and professional alike, in underwater archaeology. All this activity is licensed, co-ordinated and supervised by the central Direction de Recherches Archéologiques Sous Marines (DRASM), headed by the leading underwater archaeologist, Patrice Pomey. Although the system is very efficient and productive, the French are unhappy with it, and are in the course of tightening it up. The European Council is trying to propose solutions in the form of positive legislation, which would serve as a model for the different nations to follow.

Above all, its seems a matter of education, as the Archaelogical Centre in Gerona, Spain, has recognized; of making the general public, and especially the young generation of would-be divers, more conscious of the important role they may play in discovering and preserving their own heritage, and of persuading them to co-operate more closely with the scientists. It is felt that some of the laws concerning salvage should be applied to underwater archaeological finds. Time is indeed a major factor: each year thousands of new divers are joining in, commercial use of the shores and the sea bottom is increasing, and accelerated development, affecting the patterns of coastal sedimentation, is exposing finds which have been covered for thousands of years, and are now in imminent danger from both man and the destructive force of the sea itself.

The profession is concentrating on new techniques – penetrating and side-scanning sonars and other sensory equipment – which must be developed further and be more widely used, if it is not to rely so heavily on random finds. Saturated diving for a prolonged period of time, out of submarines, is the great hope for the future, as most of the undisturbed wrecks lie in water too deep for regular diving. The problem of preservation has also to be solved, as existing methods are very costly and time consuming, and many a find is left underwater after being studied because of the impracticality of raising and preserving it.

# MARITIME LEGISLATION TODAY

The main concern of contemporary maritime law is the harmonization of local and regional maritime legislation, such as port tariffs, marine salvage operations, and the development of transhipment ports. In 1959, the UN set up a specialized agency to deal with maritime affairs – it is the International Maritime Organization (IMO) – which has developed several significant instruments of co-operation in matters such as the prevention of collisions at sea, the prevention of pollution from ships, traffic separation schemes, safety zones around offshore structures, and the safety of life at sea.

Another UN agency, the Conference on Trade and Development (UNCTAD), deals with issues of a more economic nature:

– The present overcapacity and continuing imbalance between supply and demand, both in shipping and in shipbuilding.

– The conditions for the registration of ships, aiming at a genuine link between the flag state and the ship, in liability and the participation of nationals of the flag state in ownership and manning, in order to overcome the so called Panhonlibco (Panama, Honduras, Liberia, Costa Rica) syndrome.

– The Code of Conduct for Liner Conferences, based on the 40–40–20 principle, which gives the right to shipping lines of both exporting and importing countries to carry 40 per cent of the total traffic; 20 per cent is allowed for shipping lines of other countries.

– Measures to promote an increase in the participation of the developing countries in world shipping, in both the liner and bulk sectors.

On the highest level, the new law of the sea is trying to solve, by deliberation and legislation, political problems which are, or will shortly be, a source of friction. Central among them is the concept of territorial waters and the extent of a state's coastal jurisdiction. This concept was established hundreds of years ago on the basis of the visible horizon and later of cannon range, as extending to one nautical league (three nautical miles, a nautical mile being 1,850 m, with slight national variations). In the new law of the sea, the definition includes additional zones: territorial sea rights over 12 nautical miles, with another stretch of 12 nautical miles of Contiguous Zone, and 200 nautical miles of Exclusive Economic Zone. Other novel definitions followed: the extent of the continental shelf and continental margin, beyond the 200 nautical miles of the EEZ; special provisions for international straits, for archipelagic states, for landlocked and geographically disadvantaged states; a detailed regime for deep sea mining; the recognition of historical rights and the machinery for the settlement of disputes.

## APPENDIX D

# DIVING, HYPERBARIC MEDICINE
# AND DEEP SEA PROBES

Underwater pressure increases by one atmosphere (1 kg per 1 square cm) every ten m, so the greatest difference is felt at the beginning of the descent. At this point, when scuba-diving, pressures have to be equalized mainly in the ear by a simple act of 'pumping' the Eustachian tube. The main problems for divers arise from the simple fact that, under pressure, gases dissolve much better in fluid, so the blood holds much more gas than it normally contains. Returning to sea-level pressure, these gases form dangerous bubbles, which can cause pain, paralysis and death. This is 'the bends' or decompression sickness, the diver's worst enemy. In order to avoid it, diving is practised today according to carefully calculated decompression tables,

*Salvage methods, old and new:* (below, left and right) *ancient methods of salvage and dredging, seventeenth century;* (opposite, left) *the modern version of the same, only reaching greater depths;* (opposite, right) *the French Project Saga*

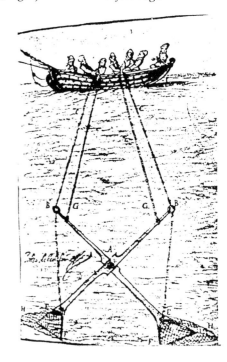

devised to decrease the pressure gradually and release the gases without causing any harm. Increased concentrations of carbon-dioxide in the system also have various negative consequences. Below 40–60 m, there is a danger of nitrogen narcosis, which induces hallucinations and is the source of such stories as divers talking to fish; it can have fatal results.

Hyperbaric medicine deals with the diver's physiopathology under the physical laws of pressure. Its main instrument is the pressure chamber, which ranges in size from the one-man emergency tank to a compact hospital. In the hyperbaric room, an atmospheric pressure higher than normal may be created by a system of compressors and safety-valves. Experiments today may be conducted in very large chambers, abyssal simulators, which can reach pressures up to 50 atmospheres, equal to a depth of 500 m. Beyond its immediate aim – to prevent the pathological consequences of uncontrolled diving – it takes advantage of the general therapeutic qualities of oxygen-rich pressurized treatment, which destroys anaerobic microbes and heals some hitherto incurable diseases. Like modern diving itself, hyperbaric medicine was first developed for military naval use, but is turning into an important tool for the general health of humanity. Besides hyperbaric medicine, institutes of marine

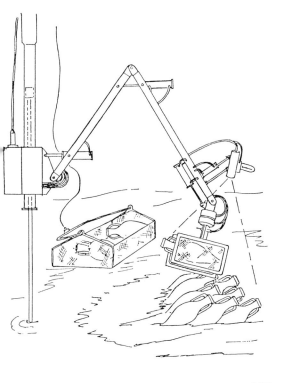

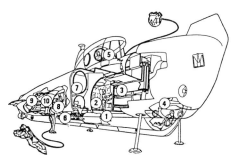

*The Saga:*

1. *Atmospheric compartment*
2. *Steering cabin*
3. *Resting area*
4. *Viewing point*
5. *Expandable steering sphere*
6. *Motor*
7. *Oxygen storage*
8. *Divers' control point*
9. *Divers' compartment*
10. *Transfer area*

medicine around the Mediterranean deal with sea-sickness and affiliated problems, with drug-consumption in port-cities and lately with the connection between AIDS and tourism.

Hardly two generations have passed since the first trials of the aqualung, and divers now can go down to 200–300 m, usually on saturated dives (staying under conditions of high pressure before and after the dive). About the same time has passed since the pioneering feats of the Piccards (father and son) with their bathyscaph, and mini research submarines are now able to reach depths of thousands of metres. However, Leonardo da Vinci wrote in his treatise on water at the end of the fifteenth century – 'Remember, when discoursing about water, to adduce first experience and then reason' – and this is still true today. In the short range, the future seems to lie with remote-control solutions, such as the Alcoa Seaprobe of Willard Bascom which, controlled from the surface, can perform delicate work at a depth of 5,000 m and more.

# FURTHER READING

*Chapter 1*   AFTER TETHYS

ADAMS, C.G. and AGER, D.V., *Aspects of Tethyan Biogeography*, London, 1967

DROOGER, C.W., ed., *Messinian Events in the Mediterranean*, Amsterdam, 1973

MASTERS, P.M. and FLEMMING, N.C., eds. *Quarternary Coastlines and Marine Archaeology*, Academic Press, London, 1983

MAVOR, J.W., Jr., *Voyage to Atlantis*, New York, 1969

RENFREW, C., *Before Civilization*, London, 1973

STANLEY, D.J., ed., *The Mediterranean Sea*, Stroudsburg, Pennsylvania, 1972

TRUMP, D.H., *The Prehistory of the Mediterranean*, Yale University Press, 1980


*Chapter 2*   THE FISH HUNT

BARDACH, J.E. et al., eds., *Fish Behaviour and its use in the Capture and Culture of Fish*, Manila, 1980

BELL, F.W., *Food from the Sea: the economics and politics of ocean fisheries*, Boulder, 1978

CORCORAN, T.H., *The Roman Fishing Industry of the Late Republic and Early Empire*, University Microfilms, Michigan, 1985

DREMIERE, P.Y. and NEDELEC, V., *Data on Fishing Vessels and Gear in the Mediterranean*, General Fisheries Council for the Mediterranean, 1977

FAO, *Atlas of the Living Resources of the Seas*, Rome, 1972

LEVI, D. and TROADEC, J.D., *The Fish Resources of the Mediterranean and Black Sea*, GFCM, 1974

RADCLIFFE, W., *Fishing from the Earliest Times*, London, 1921


*Chapter 3*   THE WATER'S EDGE

BARNIGAN, J.J. and JARRETT, H.R., eds., *The Mediterranean Lands*, London, 1975

BASLOW, M.H., *Marine Pharmacology*, New York, 1977

MANN-BORGESE, E., ed., *Pacem in Maribus*, New York, 1972

MERO, J.L., *The Mineral Resources of the Sea*, UNESCO, 1965

SINGER, C. et al., *A History of Technology*, Oxford, 1955–60

SPANIER, E., *The Royal Purple and the Biblical Blue: the study of Chief Rabbi Isaac Herzog and recent scientific contributions*, Jerusalem, 1987

UNEP, *Directory of Mediterranean Marine Research Centers*, Geneva 1977 and supplements

UNEP, *Mediterranean Action Plan*, Athens, 1985


*Chapter 4*   THE WAY OF A SHIP

BASS, G., ed., *A History of Seafaring based on Underwater Archaeology*, London, 1972

CASSON, L., *Ships and Seamanship in the Ancient World*, Princeton, 1971

FROST, H., *Under the Mediterranean: marine antiquities*, London, 1963

HAWS, D., *Ships and the Sea: a chronological review*, New York, 1975

LANDSTROM, B., *Sailing ships: from papyrus boats to full-riggers*, London, 1969

MEIJER, F., *A History of Seafaring in the Classical World*, London, 1986

THROCKMORTON, P., *Shipwrecks and Archaeology*, New York, 1969

UNGER, R.W., *The Ship in the Medieval Economy*, Montreal, 1980

*Chapter 5*   GATEWAYS AND HAVENS

FLEMMING, N., *Cities in the Sea*, New York, 1971

HOLUM, K.G. et al., *King Herod's Dream: Caesarea on the sea*, New York, 1988

KARMON, Y., *Ports Around the World*, New York, 1980

MALKIN, I. and HOHLFELDER, R.L., eds., *Mediterranean Cities: historical perspectives*, Mediterranean Historical Review, special issue, London, 1988

RABAN, A., *The Harbours of Caesarea Maritima*, Oxford, 1988

Idem, ed., *Harbour Archeology*, Oxford, 1984

*Chapter 6*   THE GREAT EXCHANGE

ASHTOR, E., *Levant Trade in the Later Middle Ages*, Princeton, 1983

BREA, B.L., *Sicily before the Greeks*, London, 1966

CULICAN, W., *The First Merchant Venturers*, London, 1966

D'ARMS, J.H. and KOPFF, E.C., eds., *The Seaborne commerce of Ancient Rome*, Rome, 1980

FAO, *Report of the Olive Cultivation in the Countries of the Mediterranean Basin and the Near East*, No. TA 3195, Rome, 1974

FEARNLY, S., *World Bulk Trade*, Oslo, 1986

FORBES, R.J., *Metallurgy in Antiquity*, Leiden, 1950

GRACE, V., *Amphoras and the Ancient Wine Trade*, Princeton, 1961

*International Petroleum Encyclopaedia*, Tulsa, 1982

LUCIANI, G., ed., *The Mediterranean Region, Economic Interdependence and the Future of Society*, London, 1984

*Chapter 7*   STEERING TO THE HORIZON

CARY, M. and WARMINGTON, E., *The Ancient Explorers*, New York, 1929

DEACON, G.E.R., ed., *Seas, Maps and Men*, New York, 1962

HILL, H.O. et al., *Instruments of Navigation: a catalogue of the National Maritime Museum*, London, 1958

MAY, W.E. and HOLDER, L., *A History of Marine Navigation*, New York, 1973

PRINS, A.H.J., *In Peril on the Sea, Marine Votive Paintings in the Maltese Islands*, Valletta, 1989

*Sailing Directions for the Mediterranean*, US Navy, Hydrographic Office, Washington

TAYLOR, E., *The Haven-Finding Art: a history of navigation from Odysseus to Captain Cook*, 2nd edition, London, 1971

*Weather in the Mediterranean*, Meteorological Office, Air Ministry, Great Britain, 2nd edition, London, 1962

*Chapter 8*   LIFE ON BOARD

CASSON, L., *The Ancient Mariners*, London, 1959

Idem, *Travel in the Ancient World*, London, 1969

FRICKE, P., *Seafarer and community*, London, 1973

LANE, F.C., *Venice and History*, Baltimore, 1973

MOREBY, D.H., *Personnel Management in Merchant Ships*, Oxford, 1968

NEWTON, A.P., ed., *Travels and Travellers of the Middle Ages*, London, 1926

PRESCOTT, H.F.M., *The Jerusalem Journey: pilgrimage to the Holy Land in the fifteenth century*, London, 1954

SAPORI, A., *The Italian Merchants in the Middle Ages*, New York, 1970


*Chapter 9*   THE LAW OF THE SEA

ASHBURNER, W., *The Rhodian Sea Law*, Oxford, 1909

COLOMBUS, C.J., *International Law of the Sea*, London, 1968

JADOS, S.S., *Consulate of the Sea and Related Documents*, Alabama, 1975

LOPEZ, R.S. and RAYMOND, I.W., *Medieval Trade in the Mediterranean World*, New York, 1955

*The Mediterranean in the New Law of the Sea*, Foundation for International Studies, Malta, 1987

PRESCOTT, J.R.V., *The Maritime Political Boundaries of the World*, London, 1985

TRUVER, S.C., *The Strait of Gibraltar and the Mediterranean*, Germantown, Maryland, USA, 1980


*Chapter 10*   THEATRE OF WAR

CURREY, E.H., *Sea Wolves of the Mediterranean: the grand period of the modern corsairs*, London, 1910

FISHER, SIR G., *Barbary Legend: war, trade and piracy in North Africa, 1415–1830*, Westport, 1974

MAHAN, A.T., *The Influence of Sea Power upon History, 1660–1783*, London, 1965

ORMEROD, H.A., *Piracy in the Ancient World: an essay in Mediterranean history*, Liverpool, 1924

PRYOR, J.H., *Geography, Technology and War: studies in the maritime history of the Mediterranean, 649–1571*, Cambridge University Press, 1988

REYNOLDS, C.G., *Command of the Sea, the History and Strategy of Maritime Empires*, New York, 1974

TENENTI, A., *Piracy and the Decline of Venice*, London, 1967

VAN DE SOUTHWORTH, J., *The Age of Sails: the story of naval warfare under sail, 1213–1853*, New York, 1968

Idem, *The Ancient Fleets: the story of naval warfare under oars, 2600 BC–1597 AD*, New York, 1968


*Chapter 11*   WAVES OF MIGRATION

ATTENBOROUGH, D., *The First Eden*, London, 1987

BOARDMAN, J., *The Greeks Overseas*, Baltimore, 1964

BRADFORD, E., *The Mediterranean: a portrait of a sea*, London, 1971

BRAWDON, S.G.F., ed., *Ancient Empires*, London, 1970

BRAUDEL, F., *The Mediterranean and the Mediterranean World in the Age of Philip II*, 1949, English edition: London, 1972

CARRINGTON, R., *The Mediterranean: cradle of western culture*, New York, 1971

CURTIN, F.D., *Cross-Cultural Trade in World History*, Cambridge University Press, 1984

GOITEIN, S.D., *A Mediterranean Society: The Jewish communities of the Arab world as portrayed in the documents of the Cairo Geniza*, Los Angeles, 1967–83

GORDON, C.H., *Before the Bible: the common background of Greek and Hebrew civilizations*, London, 1962

MOSCATI, S., *The World of the Phoenicians*, London, 1968

PINKELE, C.F. and POLLIS, A., *The Contemporary Mediterranean World*, New York, 1983


*Chapter 12*   THE CALL OF THE SEA

BASCOM, W., *Deep Water, Ancient Ships: the treasure vault of the Mediterranean*, New York, 1976

COUSTEAU, J., *Man Reenters the Sea*, New York, 1974

Idem, *The Silent World*, London, 1953

FLEMMING, N., ed., *The Undersea*, London, 1977

SEMPLE, E.C., *The Geography of the Mediterranean Region and its Relation to Ancient History*, New York, 1971

# NOTES AND ACKNOWLEDGEMENTS

## Chapter 1

All quotations from the Old and New Testaments are from the King James version of the Bible.

All translations from classical sources are according to the *Loeb Classical Library*, unless otherwise indicated.

## Chapter 4

p. 56: Venice Archive and P. Bembo, *Letters*, quoted and translated by E. Concina, 'Humanism on the Sea', in *Mediterranean Cities: historical perspectives*, a special issue of *Mediterranean Historical Review* 3/1988, pp. 159–165, by permission of Frank Cass and Company

## Chapter 5

p. 70: AlMaqdisī, *Ahsan at-taqāsīm fi marifat alaqālīm*, ed. De Goeje, Leiden, 1906, p. 163; English translation by G. Le Strange, *Palestine Under the Moslems*, London, 1890, pp. 328–9

p. 72: Dante Alighieri, *La divina commedia*, *Inferno*, 21, translation by H.W. Longfellow, Boston, 1884, p. 135

## Chapter 6

p. 85: Ibn Khordadhbeh, *Kitāb almasālik walmamālik*, ed. De Goeje, Leiden, 1889, pp. 66–7; translation in R.S. Lopez and I.W. Raymond, *Medieval Trade in the Mediterranean World*, 1955, pp. 31–2 by permission of Columbia University Press, New York

p. 86: F.B. Pegolotti, *La pratica della mercatura*, ed. A. Evans, Cambridge, Massachusetts, 1936

## Chapter 7

p. 102: A. Neckham, *De Naturis Rerum*, ed. T. Wright, London, 1863, p. 183

p. 103: R.B. Motzo, *Il compasso da navigare*, 1947, p. 62 (author's translation) by permission of Cagliari University Press

## Chapter 9

p. 122: J.B. Pritchard, *Ancient Near Eastern Texts Relating to the Old Testament*, 1950, pp. 25–29 by permission of Princeton University Press

p. 124: W. Ashburner, *The Rhodian Sea-Law*, Oxford, 1909, 3:9, p. 87

p. 126: Lopez and Raymond, p. 176 by permission of Columbia University Press, New York

p. 128: ibid, p. 170 by permission of Columbia University Press, New York

p. 129: A. Udovich, *Partnership and Profit in Medieval Islam*, 1970, p. 228 by permission of Princeton University Press

p. 131: S.D. Goitein, *Letters of Medieval Jewish Traders*, 1973, p. 334 by permission of Princeton University Press

## Chapter 11

p. 159: Fulcher of Chartres, *A History of the Expedition to Jerusalem*, translated by F.R. Ryan, 1969, pp. 271–2 by permission of the University of Tennessee Press

p. 162: Lopez and Raymond, Introduction by permission of Columbia University Press, New York

## Chapter 12

p. 167: J. MacInnis, *Underwater Images: explorations of the diver's world*, 1971, pp. 7–9 by permission of the Canadian Publishers, McClelland and Stewart, Toronto

p. 172: A.H.J. Prins, *In Peril on the Sea*, 1989, p. 16 by permission of Said International Ltd, Malta

p. 172: F.C. Lane, *Venice and History* by permission of the Johns Hopkins University Press, Baltimore, 1973, p. 57

p. 174: R. Foulke, 'The Literature of Voyaging' in *Literature and Lore of the Sea* edited by Patricia Ann Carlson, 1986, p. 3, by permission of Rodopi, Amsterdam

p. 175: C. Camilleri, *Mediterranean Music*, 1988, pp. 23 and 41 by permission of the Mediterranean Institute, University of Malta

p. 176: Adunis, from *Victims of a Map* by permission of Saqi Books, London

p. 177: Y. ʼAmichai, by permission of Harper and Row, New York

## Appendix D

p. 188: J.P. Richter and C. Pedretti, *Leonardo da Vinci*, 1977, vol. II, p. 236 by permission of Phaidon Press Limited

# INDEX

Sicily (*cont.*)
  Sea People settled on, 150
  Straits of, 5, 44, 146
  volcanic activity, 16
  mentioned, 14, 63, 76, 85,
    100, 140, 151, 152, 154, 172
  *see also* names of places in
    Sicily
Sidon, 22, 96
sieges, maritime, 141
sills, 7
silting, 69
Sinai campaign (1956), 146
Sinan Pasha, 144
Sind, 86
Sirenes, 169
Sirte (Sydra), Gulf of, 6, 134
skeleton-first system, 53
slaves/slavery, 113, 116–7, 131,
  163
Slavs, 163
smuggling, 111
Smyrna, 60
soap, 41–2
soda ash, 41–2
Sofia-Antipolis, 182
solar-heat, 43
Solomon, King of Israel, 36
sonar survey, 66
Song of Solomon, 37
Sounion, Cape, 168
South Africa, 83
South America, 5
Spain
  Armada, 142
  dispute over Gibraltar, 134
  emigration from, 165
  fishing, 26, 28, 30, 32
  Jews expelled from, 162
  literature, 177
  metals, 78, 79
  oil, 33, 89
  plate movements, 5
  scholars, 104
  shipyards, 72
  soap export, 41
  tourism, 28, 35
  unification, 163
  winds, 92, 93

  wine, 83, 84
  mentioned, 9, 25, 26, 55, 56,
    91, 100, 118, 135, 151, 158,
    170, 184
  *see also* names of places in
    Spain
Spargi, 183
spices, 86
Split, 182
sponges, 38
*sposalizio*, 178
Spoleto: *Festivale dei Duo
  Mondi*, 178
springs, submarine freshwater,
  43
square sail, 55
steam, 56, 141
steel, 56, 141
steering, 54–5
Steffy, Richard, 49
stern rudder, 54–5, 58
Stone Age, 12
stone quarries, 39
stoppers, amphorae, 83
Stromboli, 16
submarines, 56, 58, 147–8
submergence, 69
subsidence, 68, 178
Suez, 86, 146
  Canal, 16, 29, 40, 72, 87, 89,
    101, 146, 165
Sulcis, 152
SuMed pipeline, 89
supercarriers, 56
supertankers, 89
surface fish, 19, 20, 31
Sveti Stefan, 35
Syracuse, 64, 141
Syria, 5, 45, 47, 61, 86, 151,
  163, 165
Syrian–African rift, 4
Syrians, 85
Syro–Palestinian coast, 78, 150

Tabat-elHamman, 61
Talmud, 22
Tanin, 13
Tanit, 154, 168, 171
Tarragona, 157

Tarshish, 78
Tarsos, 78
Tasman Sea, 6
Tavola de Martelojo, 105
technological progress, 42, 53
Tel-Nami, 60
temples, 154, 170
tenon-and-mortise joint, 47
Terra Amata, 12
Terracina, 51
territorial waters, concept of,
  185
terrorism, 148
Tethys, 4, 5, 6
Texas A & M University, 183
textiles, 86
Thasos, 83, 143
Thebes, 126
Thera, 14–15, 16, 40, 48–9
three-mile zone, 30
Throckmorton, Peter, 77, 183
Thucydides, 154
Tiahamat, 13
Tiber, River, 80
Tiberius, Emperor, 80
timber, 86
Timna Egyptian mines, 79
tin, 77, 78, 79, 93
Tiraz, 38
Titan, 183
*Titanic*, 58
Tjeker, 122
Tohu, 13
Toledo, 158
Tophet, 152
torpedoes, 141
Torre del Greco, 39
Tortosa, 78
tourism, 28–9, 34, 149
trade, 60, 61, 62, 76–90, 129 *see
  also* merchants
Trani, 124
Transjordan, 139
TransMed line, 89
transom stern, 54
travel memoirs, 177
trenches, 6, 7
Trimalchio, 81
Tripoli, 118